CHAOS UNBOUND

CHAOS UNBOUND
A Jewish Childhood in Nazi Berlin

Elaine V. Siegel

Keynote Books, LLC   Montclair, NJ   2013

© 2013 Elaine V. Siegel

Library of Congress Control Number: 2012953070

10 9 8 7 6 5 4 3 2 1

All rights reserved. No part of this publication may be reproduced, stored in a retrieval system, or transmitted, in any form or by any means, electronic, mechanical, photocopying, recording, or otherwise, without the written permission of Keynote Books, LLC. For information write: Keynote Books, LLC, P.O. Box 43238, Upper Montclair, NJ 07043; email: info@keynote-books.com.

ISBN: 978-0-9830807-4-9

Book design and production: Andrea Schettino

*This book is dedicated to
the memory of my grandmother, Anna Schnell,
who taught me how much a loving family protects
one from the vicissitudes of life. Her love continues
to live through me and on to my daughter,
Anita, and my granddaughter, Tamara.*

Contents

Prologue . . . . *xi*

Introduction . . . . *xiii*

Ch 1:   A Strong Foundation. 3

Ch 2:   Beyond My Front Door 33

Ch 3:   The Unraveling. 45

Ch 4:   Lives Transformed. 51

Ch 5:   A Misfit 57

Ch 6:   Life is a Circus 65

Ch 7:   Broadening Horizons 79

Ch 8:   My Mother the Bride. 93

Ch 9:   The Letzes' Garden 105

Ch 10:   Mother's Dream Come True 121

Ch 11:   A New Path. 135

Ch 12:   A Passport. 145

Ch 13:   Occupation. 155

Ch 14:   Arrival. 169

AFTERNOON

After noon it became very hot,
So I went down to the docks
Far down away by the water.
Feeling like I was at the out-
Bounds of space and town,
I saw the seagulls reeling and dealing
Their crying calls.
The waves slapped quietly around the swollen wood and
I looked down into the water
But didn't even see myself.
So I lay back and became
In my mind
Indistinguishable from the sky;
Vast, penetrable, unending.
But then I wanted my body back.
Besides, the sun was getting low
And other things were waiting

A poem by Melanie

PROLOGUE

Chaos Unbound is an account of a childhood at the threshold of chaos, of *my* childhood. Neither the occasional need to disguise this or that particular nor the novelistic quality of the storytelling alters the nature of these reflections. This is a truthful account – my truthful account – of a Jewish childhood in Berlin in the 1930s and 1940s. Certain questions posed in the writing remain unanswerable, whereas other questions came to reveal a truth previously unknown to me through the writing. I hope readers will join me in pondering the imponderable, in raising questions answerable and unanswerable, in comprehending my truths, and hopefully in discovering truths of their own.

During the 30 years over which this book was gestating, I met a great many generous people who became my friends and who over time shared their own eventful life histories with me. In learning about their pasts, I often assumed the position of a social scientist studying a particular group of subjects. But, unlike a social scientist, I allowed myself to enter into close and sometimes emotionally charged relationships with my "subjects," my friends, that lasted many years. There are too many such people to list, but if any of them are still alive, or if their children chance to read this book, they will recall cozy and animated evening conversations that were repeated over many years. Dear friends, I thank you.

Outstanding in this group is Paul Stepansky, whom I gratefully acknowledge as the most helpful editor and publisher in the world. I single out as well Diane Krasnick, who helped shape the manuscript that evolved over these many years.

Introduction

Ever since I returned to the United States more than eight decades ago, people from various walks of life have exhorted me to write about my childhood in Berlin under the Nazi regime. But I wanted nothing to do with it. Talking about IT held a hidden danger for me. It allowed the past to rush into the present with all the force of water destined to produce electricity. Words made memories of my childhood in Berlin unbearably real, transposing the pain of the past into the present. Despite my pleas to let it all go, my future American in-laws and their extended family in particular kept asking questions. No, I would tell them, I needed to distance myself from the deadly fog of those years. Yet, under cover of their affection for my husband-to-be, who was, after all, their favorite son, brother, and cousin, they kept trying to cut through the barbed wire fence I erected around my life in Germany.

I clung to the naïve conviction that I could *wegschweigen* (undo by silence) all that happened without being specific about just what I needed to hide. I yearned to be free of the constant nagging shame that made my inner life so bitter, and permitted all and sundry to sit in judgment of me. After all, none of the really nightmarish things that had temporarily shaken the conscience of the so-called civilized world had happened to me. Still, an intermittent, indistinct voice in my head acted as prosecutor, amassing evidence of my guilt. Not that I had any notion of what I stood accused. When my new relatives asked how I managed to survive, I heard: "Why are you still alive?" I asked myself the same question over and over, driven to rumination by a mother who, early in my life, had freighted me with her perception that I was ungrateful and a burden.

I secretly hoped that my escape to the wonderful country of my birth would relieve me of these nagging feelings of shame and ingratitude. My young husband-to-be did his best to shore up my self-esteem, and to a certain extent he succeeded. His support enabled me consciously to adopt a pose of superiority that tied into my mother's prejudice regarding Americans' ostensible lack of manners and culture. Some people who knew me then remember the youthful Elaine Siegel as haughty. But that was only on the outside. Inside I was quaking in vague fear of another disaster of unknown origin. And it soon materialized.

As my wedding day approached, we received a message from the Rabbi of my new family: He found that he could not perform the wedding ceremony for us because no real proof existed that I was indeed Jewish! I was devastated, my husband-to-be was furious, and my future mother-in-law cried and begged me to tell this Holy Man "the whole, real story." She did not know that she asked the one thing I simply could not provide at that point in my life. My silence only exacerbated my shame: I convinced myself that somehow everyone knew something evil about me that would soon destroy everything. After all, I had heard my mother-in-law tell one of her cronies that she had begun to share the Rabbi's suspicions: I had no concentration camp tattoo on my wrist, nor did I speak Yiddish. And further, how could I possibly be a respectable refugee when I had been born in the United States? No *yiddisher kop* (no one with Jewish "smarts") would even think of going to live in Germany in those years, she insisted.

This line of talk surfaced often enough to persuade me that I was right to refuse to talk about the genocide perpetrated by Hitler. I was constantly looking over my shoulder, afraid that something or someone would wrest my birthright, my American citizenship, away from me. And I had to agree: On the surface, returning to Germany in 1931 *did* seem unreasonable. How could my prospective in-laws know that my mother was actually known for her madcap ways? When she decided to rejoin her mother and her Swiss stepfather, she was intent on building a new life in Germany. And Germany, she was convinced, was ripe for change.

In my later years, looking back on a rich life full of love, children, and success, I was able to let surface some anecdotes about the years in Germany. These spontaneous eruptions favored the satiated time right after a luncheon or dinner party with friends, when hunger was vanquished and the atmosphere allowed for a cozy intimacy. People close to me couldn't get enough of the stories I told. So the question of writing a book came up again. Friends and family pointed out that I might be one of the last surviving members of a group who lived in Hitler's cannon-infested German mansion, all the while remaining convinced that the tenets of the *Sozialdemokratische Arbeiterpartei* (the social democratic worker's union) constituted the only hope of betterment for all Germans.

Despite the vast schism between Americans' and Germans' understanding of wealth, there was an unspoken pact between victors and vanquished that culminated in the Marshall Plan. As the war ended, the United States had yet to encounter – or even to imagine the existence of –a dynamic worldview, a *Weltanschauung,* that valued death. This naiveté resulted in the great optimism that followed the end of hostilities. Despite the discovery of the death camps, this optimism allowed wounds of the soul to begin to heal. Therefore, I was astounded when, after my emigration, my American friends discussed many of the same socioeconomic issues that I had grown up with. I often chimed in during long philosophical and political discussions, offering illustrations from my own life and referring to the unusual personae that populated it.

As I matured and completed professional training, my

writings attracted the interest of various faculties in the humanities. When I travelled to discuss my work, anecdotes from my years in Berlin proved a great drawing card, even in Berlin itself, where I returned to lecture only with the greatest reluctance. Back in Germany, now a psychologist and psychoanalyst, I did not hide my true self as I had as a child. Quite the opposite: I wanted to tell all about my childhood in Berlin; I wanted audiences to take in my experiences. As a lecturer, I was always concerned that my audiences would enjoy my style of storytelling more than they would be moved to reflection by the content of my stories. The word "charming" was used often by those who came to know me. But for me the word had a deadly ring. There were few things "charming" in Hitler's Berlin, the Berlin of my childhood.

After a while it dawned on me that the distortions in my family's value system and the corrosive conflicts among family members mirrored Hitler's perversions, which not only poisoned several generations of Germans but also made them unable to mourn, as the German psychoanalyst Alexander Mitscherlich pointed out. There was a mutually agreed upon silence during the Hitler years; it cut people off from their families and forced them to give up leadership roles in their communities. Surely, I thought at long last, something could be learned by my retelling what I remembered. At 80 years of age, why should I still be afraid of my childhood?

Another less obvious message reached me and persuaded me to undertake the task of setting painful memories to paper. After World War II, the United States of America was indeed a marvelous country. It underwrote the rebuilding of what the war had destroyed and it inspired high hopes of lasting world peace. I was proud to be an American and wanted to contribute what I could, if only in the form of a record of personal experiences for the benefit of family and friends, professional colleagues, and historians of Germany and World War II. Once I allowed the memories to surface, they washed over me like storm clouds, overriding my desire for an orderly chronology of particulars. Therefore, I decided to focus upon individuals, their relationships to me, and how each one of them handled the deeply existential dilemma of living in Hitler's Reich.

Here then are those individuals who shaped my development, either directly or by example. First and foremost, there was my maternal grandmother, Anna Schnell Schwager. Anna had been married twice. Her first husband was Jakob Resco. They had one daughter, Charlotte, my mother, who later married Fred Letz, my biological father. Anna's second husband, who joined her in caring for me after my return to Berlin, was Ferdinand Schwager. A Swiss citizen living in Berlin, Ferdinand considered it a privilege to support my mother and me.

Oma (grandmother) Anna was the first person I met who was willing and able to talk to me about my father. He was, she told me, an extraordinarily good-looking man, but nature did not give him an equally imposing body. He was very short and suffered daily, convinced that his short stature blocked the success he was entitled to. He was the first person in his family to attend a *Gymnasium* (the traditional German high school), as he was given a scholarship. His family would have been unable to pay even the relatively low tuition fee. And he was also a good dancer, invited to all "the best houses" at party time. His mother, my paternal grandmother Amanda, complained bitterly that his friendly social contacts all forgot about him when it came time for him to find employment.

My parents knew each other from kindergarten on. They had met shortly after their respective families, the Rescos and the Letzes, had moved to Berlin where the young husbands sought to make their fortunes. Neither was very successful, and my father, Fred, turned to politics. Charlotte and Fred became fast friends after they were mobbed by a group of bullies. No one expressed surprise when, sometime later, they announced their engagement. Shortly after the engagement was announced, my father left for the United States; perhaps he sought to lay down roots in a kinder and gentler environment. My mother, then a girl of 18, was unwilling to await his return. She sold every one of their engagement gifts and went off to the U.S. on an old steamer that carried all of eight passengers. She was the only female passenger and, being a very handsome young woman, was continually besieged by crew and fellow travelers alike. She stayed in the United States just long enough to produce a daughter and left exclaiming, "Who is this butcher, baker, and candlestick maker to think himself as good as me?"

My mother and I set sail from New York and arrived in Berlin in the summer of 1931. I was all of two and a half years old. It was initially assumed by both sets of grandparents that we had come in order to become acquainted with one another. After all, I was the first grandchild; how fortunate, they thought, that my father was successful enough to send his wife and daughter back to Germany for a visit. Many of their neighbors and friends who had emigrated from Germany were never heard from again. Older folks learned of the birth of grandchildren only when one or another émigré washed out and returned home, in debt to the government for his or her passage. The fairytale land with streets of gold had not kept its promise for many. Better to come back, they thought, and join the bread and soup lines where they at least knew the language and, often enough, one another.

My relatives insisted that I couldn't possibly remember our arrival in Germany from America. I was too little, they said. But I do remember. The sensations I experienced made a deep impression on me even though years would pass before I could name the emotions my relatives and I felt on being united. My cheeks were wet because a great many relatives felt they needed to kiss me. "A real American in our family," some said with wonderment. My cheeks were also burned and red as my great uncles could not refrain from pinching them in enthusiastic approval of my well-fed state. They didn't think that people ate properly "on the outside." Later, I pondered whether my great uncles meant literally outside of Germany or simply outside the bounds of Kashrut, the Jewish dietary laws. I was frightened by this strange throng. I couldn't understand a word they said, for in America we had spoken only English.

Overwhelmed with all these strange-speaking, aggressively affectionate people, I did the only thing I could: I screamed and cried. Mother tried to hush me and pointed out that my tears were falling on my starched organdy dress and were making it go limp. I looked around, hoping my father would appear. When he didn't, I allowed my paternal grandfather, Christian Letz, to pick me up. He and my paternal grandmother Margarete Tiedke Letz (Oma Amanda) lived close by and made sure to stay connected with me throughout my childhood. In addition to their son, my father Fred, they had had a daughter who died in childhood. The fact that they were observant Christians who belonged to a charismatic sect made for an interesting dynamic with my maternal grandparents.

In the years to follow, my two best friends were Helga Musterweg and Pauli Gracieli, with whom I shared virtually all of my childhood experiences. Other important influences were Mother Gräfchen, my babysitter; Nataly Ingelmeier, our landlady; Mathias auf der Heyde, my Oma (grandmother) Anna's and my friend and outing companion; Herr Herbst, a good teacher and a good Nazi; my stepfather, Waldemar Friedrich von Udebek, and the Udebek clan that surrounded him; and Herr Schloske, the Udebek's Man Friday and driver. This small group was my universe. It colored my perceptions and created the young woman who left Germany in 1946 to seek a new life in America.

CHAOS UNBOUND

chapter one
A STRONG FOUNDATION

Anna Schnell, my maternal grandmother, was without a doubt the most important person in my life. She, more than my mother, shaped what I actually perceived of the world into a value system I can live with, even now. At first, it was confusing all right. Here was a lady who later seemed demented, who always told me the truth while all around me Hitler's giant propaganda machine turned families into spy organizations, gave current events an information spin that makes modern election campaign practices seem guileless, and entrusted policing of the so-called Thousand Year Empire to thugs and murderers. All this occurred while Hitler himself became the prototype of genocidal tyrants. But I am way ahead of the narrative.

Anna was relatively tall for a woman of her generation, full-breasted with the large, flat, bunioned feet of a peasant, and a slight limp. I had heard that she was once ill with a bad case of pneumonia and had to stay in bed. She refused to use the bedpan, to everyone's surprise. After all, she had been brought

Anna Schwager, née Anna Schnell, as a young woman around the turn of the century

up on a farm on the then Polish border of Germany where even a chamber pot was considered a refinement few could afford. Anyway, Anna needed to relieve herself and was carried to the toilet by her second husband, Ferdinand Schwager. One Sunday, after he returned from his weekly Sunday morning beer swilling, he hoisted her on his back and stumbled, somehow catching her leg on the door frame and twisting her hip socket out of alignment. It never healed properly. She was left with a gentle sway while walking, reminiscent of an aroused swan beating her wings against unruly waters.

Nobody told me this straight on. I heard several versions of the accident while sitting in the womblike embrace of the long, hand-embroidered tablecloth that always covered the round coffee table in the living room nook. The version favored by Anna herself recounted Ferdinand's utter devotion during her illness. He made a bed tray for her, covered it all over with painted white flowers, and served her meals in bed. He wanted to hire a nurse or at least a charwoman, but Anna would have none of it. She claimed it would have been a waste of money.

But I, hiding under the coffee table, comfortably protected from the ladies who came for cake and coffee – and thus safe from pinched cheeks, kisses from malodorous mouths, and suffocating embraces – thought there might be more to the accident. The grown-ups talked about it too often and did not relegate it to the "stories to be told" pile of their repertoire of entertaining stories. My other grandmother, the Christian

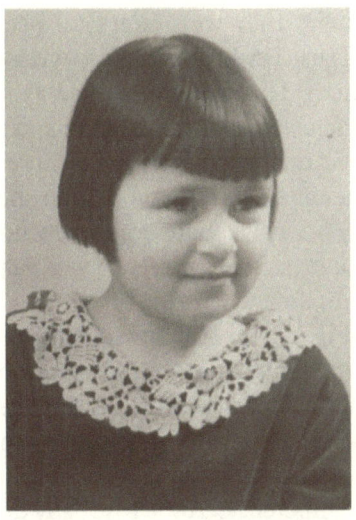

Elaine Siegel, née Elaine Letz, age 4, in 1933,
about 18 months after her return to Berlin

one, Margarete Tietkge Letz (Oma Amanda), thought Ferdinand must have been drunk – "as usual," she added. How could a grown man twist his wife's leg right out of its socket without her shouting for help or groaning with pain, she wondered. The door was a large one, painted a gleaming white with a large brass handle and carved frame. According to

Oma Amanda, the accident could only have happened if either Ferdinand were dead drunk or raving mad. But Anna only smiled and poured more coffee.

Her friends often delicately asked how the hip was and suggested it might be too much for her to have to take care of a wild American grandchild. Anna smiled and poured more coffee. She didn't think I was wild, just high spirited and enthusiastic, for which she claimed to be grateful. After all, she explained, I was never bored and was disobedient only when treated unfairly.

Anna's friends didn't buy it and neither did Oma Amanda. Perhaps, I thought, they were skeptical because of Anna's religion, and because Ferdinand, her second husband, was not even of her religion. I puzzled about the varying opinions and came to the conclusion that the friends and Amanda didn't understand that Anna loved Ferdinand more than she loved me or my mother and certainly more than she loved her first husband, the legendary Jakob Resco, about whom nobody ever spoke but whose mysterious presence was palpable when the talk turned to Anna's accident.

The coffee table, which so conveniently provided shelter for me during my fact-finding missions, stood in front of a huge white oven, the only means of heating the large room. It was a Berlin-style oven, all white tiles with a yellow belt of stucco grapes and large vine leaves curling around the comfortable circumference. Anna rose early during the winter months. She lit a slow fire in the guts of the white giant so that Ferdinand would be comfortable while getting ready for work. On school days, I used to run shivering into the toilet and then across the short dark corridor to that warm, mellow haven, carrying my school clothes in my arm. The other girls in my class envied me. They had no one to light the fires so early in the morning, or their families could not afford to buy coal. The design around the waist of the oven was repeated on the stuccoed ceiling that was originally festooned by kerosene lamps, later by dimly burping gas lamps. It now held an elegant electric chandelier. Ferdinand liked to be modern. Anna adored him and, as they say, he "thought the world of her." At his Sunday morning beer-drinking marathons, he couldn't boast enough about her gentle ways, superior cooking, and dedication to the family. Even when deep in his cups he never mentioned that she was Jewish or that she was active with him among the Socialists. He seemed unaware of her good looks, focusing with benevolent criticism on her lack of stylishness and disregard of modern grooming. In the 1930s, she still wore her auburn, slightly wavy, baby fine hair pinned up in a Victorian bun and favored heavy walking shoes that accommodated her broad feet. Her face was heart-shaped. High cheek-bones accentuated Slavic eyes, which were deep grey. She had a favorite saying about the color of eyes that she liked to recite while combing her hair.

> *Graue Augen sind graulich*
> *Aber ganz getreulich*
> (Grey eyes are truly grey
> But always the truth they say)

We would discuss in great detail what the color, shape, and size of eyes said about people. Anna was a natural psychologist and, under the guise of recalling myths that she made up on the spot, she would offer advice and support to the many women who came to her in time of trouble. She was a midwife, an unusual profession for a nice Jewish farmer's daughter. I'm not certain if she had formal training. But I am certain that she could, and did, help many women. I was an avid assistant. Usually, the women came first to talk to Anna, preferably when Ferdinand was at work or Sunday morning when the men frequented their *Stammtisch* (a reserved table at their favorite pub). Although I was an expert at spreading reams of newspaper on the floor and filling the warm water reservoir of the kitchen stove – also white but without ornamentation – I was not invited to be present at interviews.

This was when I developed the habit of sitting under the coffee table in order to listen to the often brutal tales Anna's patients brought her. There were tales of men pushing pregnant women down the cellar steps and then, when their bleeding started, refusing to pay for the doctor. And there were stories of men nearly choking women to death and leaving them to shiver and freeze in an attic storage room or a musty coal bin and with hardly any clothes on - all this just because the men suspected that they had a rival, which they usually did. Mostly Anna advised women to leave. But many were afraid of starving, so they went back to their men, returning to her on the next occasion when they were almost killed. This was before Hitler made jobs available to unwed mothers and gave medals to women with four or more, preferably blond, children.

By that time, Anna had to cope with men who had been beaten up, threatened, and shot at by the Brownshirts, or who found themselves at odds with the law. These men were hidden in the attic of the apartment house that was known to be populated primarily by members of the Socialist Party. There were also a few Jewish families who mainly kept to themselves. I understood that we had nothing in common with them because we rarely went to temple – I thought of it as the temple in Jerusalem, especially Solomon's Temple, the sacking of which led the oracle to predict the downfall of ancient Babylonia by writing on the wall of King Belshazzar's palace: *"Mene, Mene, Tekel, u-Pharsin"* (the handwriting is on the wall). My own religious training took place under the tablecloth because both Anna and Ferdinand were so-called free thinkers and members of the Socialist Party. Apparently "free thinking" was a requirement of membership. Later I learned – also under the table – that more likely than not, we did not go to the temple or any other religious institution because Ferdinand was a goy and did not feel comfortable in the Synagogue.

Anna never took money for her services, proudly telling the women that Ferdinand could easily support her and that she was glad she could help. She often sang ballads in a voice high and true. The ballads frequently dealt with maidens ready to drown themselves because their lovers had left or made them pregnant. Some did drown, others decided to live because their babies made them happy.

> *Oh nein, wir wollen leben*
> *Wir beide, Du und ich.*
> *Deinem Vater sei vergeben,*
> *Wie glucklich machst Du mich.*
> (Oh, no, let us live
> Both of us, you and me.
> Your father was forgiven,
> How happy you make me.)

Anna also had a large store of poetry which she would recite at appropriate and sometimes not so appropriate times. She particularly liked *Erlkönig* (Alder King) in which a child died right in his father's arms. A close second was a poem about two royal children who couldn't get together because a river separated them with currents too deep to swim across. Her recitations were dramatic and utterly convincing. I could smell the swamp the rider had to traverse and shuddered at the depth of the cold, cold water the royal youngsters could not conquer.

The thought of an early, tragic death appealed to me immensely. It would save me from having to make unpleasant decisions and also from the need to please my mother. By then, she was home only about every third or fourth weekend, descending like a tornado upon our peaceful household. It seemed peaceful to me in comparison with my mother's icy disapproval of what I thought of as "our" socialist point of view. And then there was her stern insistence that I learn how to curtsey, use all sorts of polite phrases, and know which fork to use with each course of a meal. When she decided that I should learn the fine art of kissing hands, Ferdinand dropped the fork that he was just conveying to his mouth. "What are you trying to do?" he shouted. "Make a monkey out of her?"

I knew enough to leave the table and go to the room I shared with Mother during her visits. The ensuing fight could be heard for miles around, I was sure. But I didn't mind. We heard plenty of fights every day, especially when men came home from work and dinner wasn't on the table or the children were not quiet. For many, it was a question of money to buy adequate food for the whole family. The many who were unemployed frequently came home drunk and beat up everyone in sight because they could not find work, or so it was explained to me. I did not understand the connection until I grew up and studied psychology. Back then, I accepted as fact

Elaine, age 4, with her mother in 1933

that men would not drink beer any more or beat their wives and children if only they would become socialists.

Anna and I often discussed that one of these days my mama (with the accent on the second syllable) would probably marry again. I did not understand how my mother could marry again because my father had not left us. We had left him. All of the stories I had heard dealt with men leaving women. Anyway, my father was an unknown entity far away in America, where I had been born. The story of my birth in America and my uncertain future in Germany were often discussed with friends and acquaintances. My story, told by Anna with melancholic emphasis on uncertainty and possibly one-sided love (of my unknown father for my beautiful mother) could easily qualify me as a love child and my mother as the unhappy maiden of one of Anna's ballads.

The only trouble was that my mother was not unhappy. Quite to the contrary, she was reputed to be having the time of her life since coming back to Germany. Anna was both intrigued and repelled by her daughter's actions. She herself was still struggling with the after-effects of her first marriage, as I learned under the table. Although Anna's first husband, Jakob Resco, had deserted her, she felt somehow responsible for the break-up because she was now happy in her "inconvenient" marriage to a man of a different faith, class, and nationality. I gathered that having a nationality was very difficult, something that became clear to me after listening so often to the tale of my birth, which made me feel different from other children. I was American and Mother expected me to announce this to anyone who questioned where I came from and what I was doing in Germany. Being questioned about such matters by both official and self-appointed guardians of the state was routine in those days.

It was under the tablecloth that I learned that Anna was married for a second time, and outside of her own religion. As to her first husband, Jakob Resco, she had apparently been warned by her family that he was a ladies' man and not to be trusted. But she, with her usual disregard for the majority opinion, had married him anyway and moved with him to a city called Krakow. Within the span of their first year together, she gave birth to my mother and Jakob had left her. Her in-laws wanted her to come to them with the child, but Anna refused. She returned to the parental farm, where Mother suffered nightmares that someone was about to kidnap and enslave her until the end of her days. She never allowed herself to become aware of the possible connection between the nightmares and her paternal grandparents' wishes.

Eventually, via a grapevine that snaked through most of Europe from one shtetl to another, from one rabbi to another, Anna heard that Jakob had been seen in Berlin. She left her little daughter on the farm, giving an instruction that, under no circumstances, was the child to be given to her paternal grandparents. She did not find Jakob in Berlin, and when she returned home three years later, she was legally divorced and remarried to Ferdinand. She never talked about those three years even though her family questioned and exhorted and threatened to sit shiva for her. She listened, packed up her child, and went back to Berlin. By the time my mother and I arrived from America in 1931, a reconciliation of sorts had taken place. But my mother's return was very different from Anna's earlier one. Mother wanted to build a better life that was not dependent on nationality and the power of a rich man.

As for Anna, she maintained that being German wasn't all that wonderful, given the country's political structure and the sorry German record of the First World War. She preferred her Polish affiliations, though they too were suspect because many of them were not socialists and had participated in something very bad called a "pogrom." I thought a pogrom was another of Anna's ballads, where maidens were misused by Cossacks who wore colorful uniforms and rode noble horses. The Poles also drank too much alcohol, were not Socialists but Royalists, and had no respect for anyone.

Anna wanted to agree with Ferdinand's concept of the workers of the world uniting in order to overthrow tyrannical governments. But she was not at all sure that just overthrowing a government would bring about happiness and equality. A careful plan for what to do after the overthrow was needed, she thought. Besides, she could not really make up her mind if she was German or Polish. Her birthplace was a small village which straddled the border between Germany and Poland. It was called Sbrinkov in Polish and Waldfried in German. Anna thought of herself as belonging to both groups and could not understand what all the fuss with wars and bloody surrender was about. When it finally became necessary to choose one side or the other side, she opted for a third version: She would be a citizen of the world.

Ferdinand fully approved of this idea. Anything Anna did was was just fine with him; indeed, it was perfect. And besides, there was her puzzling lack of censure and displeasure about his behavior on Sunday mornings, which he regarded as a true measure of her love for him. Anna, he intoned over and over, was the most feminine of women. He never added that she was also the kind that his type of jovial bon vivant usually found boring. And, after all, Ferdinand had his own issues about nationality. Although constantly under pressure at his place of work to become a German citizen so he could be trusted with highly specialized and supposedly secret work, he tenaciously held on to his Swiss citizenship. This seemed to allow him to maintain an inner security when voicing his socialist opinions.

Ferdinand and Anna became the inner core of those courageous enough to protest when the Brownshirts became more and more brazen and powerful. "They smell the stink of their own corruption. They are dangerous. Let's go farm, or to Switzerland," begged Anna. She had almost persuaded Ferdinand when unexpected opposition came from my mother. Mother had no intention of leaving Germany at such an exciting time, she declared, especially now that she had made the "right connections." I knew that one of the shouting matches between Ferdinand and my mother was about to erupt. Sure enough, he began to talk of socialism and declared himself wounded because Mother, whom he had nurtured in the bosom of his worker's group, not to speak of his own bosom, was about to betray all this loyalty by taking up with "bourgeois swine." Furthermore, Ferdinand wanted to know, where did she suddenly get all that money from, the money she was throwing around, buying fur coats and evening gowns when socialist comrades were rotting away in prison or had to leave the country? Mother was incensed. "You are spying on me," she shouted. "You and your idiotic messianic drivel of salvation by the proletariat. How dare you."

Ferdinand did not give an inch. It seems that Mother had taken her purchases for alteration to Mr. Levandowski, the tailor Anna knew from her village back on the border, and he had passed on the news to Ferdinand during their Sunday morning beer session. Ferdinand shouted socialist slogans and waved his arms. Mother shouted about getting bargain prices for furs to which she was definitely entitled after that awful marriage to the failure in America, and waved her arms. Anna held me in her arms and said quietly: "That failure in America, as you call him, is still the father of your child."

She thought I was upset. But I wasn't. Mother had told me often that my father in America was a failure and that was the reason why we had to come back to Germany and to live with Ferdinand and Anna until mother could make the right connections and we could have a decent life. I didn't know what she meant by "decent" but surmised it had to do with money, more money than even Ferdinand made in the factory as foreman and tool and die maker. I even knew that Mother had hired a detective to go around to all sorts of places like Krakow in Poland and Breslau in Germany and the synagogue in Sbrinkov and here in Berlin the town hall and the *Einwohneramt* (Registry for Renters and Owners of Dwellings) to delete entries about us so that we could leave these socialist drivellers and start our decent lives. We could then also forget all about the failure in America who was my father and find a new father for me. I wasn't sure I wanted a new father, especially if he had anything at all to do with the new set of polite manners I had to learn. But by now I knew it was useless to argue with my mother. She was stubborn even as a child, Anna said. But she was proven right about the driveling. Of all people to start driveling, it was Anna who began to drivel after what happened to her, and I had to take care of her instead of starting a decent life with Mother and her new connections.

Anna and Ferdinand did not approve of Mother's new connections. They kept her away from what was officially her home with us, and we often did not know where she was. Her periodic appearances were always like thunderclaps. It reminded me of the bad witches in *Snow White* and *Sleeping Beauty*. I tried to think of myself as Snow White but did not succeed. I felt I was more like the little robber girl in Hans Christian Anderson's *Snow Queen*, or like a gypsy who had been stolen from her parents' camp, in direct reversal of the usual tale in which gypsies stole a girl child who grew up to be a beautiful dancer and singer and married the richest in the land. Anna told me these stories with ever-changing nuances and was much taken by them herself. She was a wonderful companion and teacher. She used stories to inculcate in me the belief that somehow I too could make my life wonderful. Indeed, my life already had much the ring of a fairy tale, we both thought.

We speculated often about who mother's new connections could be. That they were rich was quite clear because mother now seemed to have another apartment away from us. I was not supposed to know about this but gathered as much from the general conversation between Anna and Ferdinand. He especially jeered at mother's efforts. He felt that her behavior was not suitable for the adopted daughter of a devoted socialist and working man. It detracted from his prestige, he kept yelling. Anna mildly reminded him that he was, at present, the head of the tiny group to whom he held forth, and that it was not generally known that I was his adopted daughter. But he persisted in calling the man my mother dated "a zero, not a man at all." Anna asked how he knew. He just knew, he said.

Anna seemed to be on Mother's side, never mind that Mother provoked the scorn of neighbors who felt she was spoiling herself by using make-up. To them, this seemed to have something to do with both her status as a German and as a potentially divorced woman. Wearing make-up also drew the wrath of her in-laws, my other set of grandparents, down upon her. Anna defended her daughter staunchly but my paternal grandmother, Oma Amanda, would have none of it. She felt that Mother was still her son's wife and as such had no business gallivanting around with make-up on her face. Anna pointed out that mother also held a responsible job at the bank. Oma Amanda did not think much of that either. "A foreign bank," she sneered. "She has to deal with a lot of foreigners. You should tell her to watch her step, Anna. They are not the same as we are on the outside." Anna was ready for that one. "Your son lives outside. He hasn't seen her or the child for five years." But Amanda wouldn't let go. "She should stay home and take care of the child instead of handing you the burden, at your age and in your condition." To which Anna provided a quick retort: "And what should they live on? Your son hasn't sent any money for years."

Oma Amanda turned pale and had palpitations after that. We left and didn't go back for a long time, and I would miss her. She allowed me to take some of her homeopathic medicine and led me to believe that I was normal, like everybody else. I thought of Oma Amanda and her husband as "really married," as opposed to maybe married like my mother and Anna. Their family had their share of myths too, but this chapter is about Anna. She was upset that my mother, like me, was an only child. She thought Mother wouldn't be up to so much mischief if she had a brother or sister to be with. Perhaps, I began to think, I too, another only child, was destined to a life of mischief. But Anna thought not. I was a little too precocious for my age and sometimes lazy, but basically, she gave me, as it were, a good report.

Elaine, age 6, with her paternal grandparents, Christian Letz and Margarete Teitkge Letz, in 1935

In order for Anna to maintain her supply of remedies for our family and friends, we had to go to parks and meadows at certain times in the fall when the moon was just a sliver in the sky. According to Anna, the full moon brought out the poisons in plants as well as in people. On those evenings when Ferdinand and my mother were both safely away – he with his politics, she with her new connections – we were free to go collect oak leaves, chestnuts, rose hips, nettles, and acorns. Some were cooked and rubbed into pastes, others were pickled in alcohol. Anna's larder looked like an alchemist's lair. Sometimes, the women who came for help were given some of her stock, though Anna did not like to give her medicines to just anyone. Many ascribed magic to her potions, and some turned nasty when the remedies she dispensed did not succeed.

Our neighbor, Frau Grotke, was among the nasty ones. She came to Anna when she was already "showing" though it was unclear to me just what she showed. She was one of those people who wanted to be something more than what she was, I had heard spoken under my table. She ate a lot and always took the most cake when Anna invited her cronies for afternoon coffee. It smelled delicious when she baked apple, plum or pound cake. And I heard the women speak highly of her coffee. Even under the table I could feel the atmosphere change after they had all stuffed themselves. Some kicked off their shoes, at which point I was hard-pressed not to reveal myself because the ones who made themselves comfortable without shoes smelled of unwashed stockings. Some reeked of ammonia as though they had peed on their own shoes, and some had bloody rags between their legs. The latter were the "dirt poor" ones for whom Anna felt especially sorry and was content at least to put some food in their bellies.

Frau Grotke was dirt poor but tried to hide her poverty and the fact that her husband was unemployed and even, as Ferdinand judged, unemployable. She had been a lady's maid and regaled whomever she could with tales of her former employer's elegance and wealth. She particularly liked to tell that she had gotten the job because of her own refined manner and bearing. Ferdinand grunted: "More likely an upstart hiring a show-off." But Frau Grotke stuck out her pinky when she lifted her cup and spoke *Hochdeutsch* (high German). No Berlin dialect passed her lips. The time she came while "showing" Anna sent me to my room, but I quickly crawled into my hiding place before she noticed me. Frau Grotke was crying, begging Anna to help her get rid of what was showing. Anna didn't want to. It was too late for her to remove the thing that showed. I began to surmise they were talking about a baby. I held my breath. Did Anna really know how to remove a baby? I felt the need to run, to go to the toilet.

Frau Grotke reeked of something I couldn't place. Anna tried to speak soothingly but the other woman began to wail. "It's not from him. He'll kill me if he finds out." Herr Grotke was known to beat up people. Every kid on the street had a story about seeing him pick a fight, especially on Sunday morning when the other men went to their pubs, but he lacked the money to join them. Or he would pick a fight Friday evening, when the men who had jobs came home with their pay envelopes. He was so unpleasant that even the Brownshirts so far had let him alone. "They will make people like him the Chief Enforcer," Ferdinand predicted.

I just couldn't figure out how an as yet unborn baby could make its mother happy. Clearly, this one was making its mother very unhappy. Anna gave Frau Grotke some of her herbs and told her to make a tea; maybe it would help. Later, she did not show any more. Despite this, Frau Grotke told everyone that Anna practiced medicine without a license. But that was much later, when Ferdinand's predictions had come true and Herr Grotke strutted around like a peacock in his brand new brown shirt, the Swastika on his arm, the same arm on which his wife hung adoringly.

The Grotkes deemed themselves socially significant. They

made it their task to rip out the "socially impure elements" in the neighborhood, the very thing we had been reading about in the pamphlets and booklets the Nazis had begun to distribute. They even had the grocers and butchers and bakers put one of their flyers into every order. Mr. Schmidt, the butcher, grumbled that the paper of the flyers was no good at all. It was cheap stuff and disintegrated the minute he tried to put it to use. He returned to using wax paper as the first wrap and then tidied the bundles with large brown paper. When that became too expensive, he used newspaper. Even newspaper was better than Nazi flyers. The ink on the flyers ran more than the ink on newspapers, and that, as far as he was concerned, showed conclusively that the Nazis were not only fools but ignorant fools.

Among the socially impure was Anna, the Grotkes claimed. At about this time, my chronology becomes shaky. There was a kind of tension everywhere I didn't understand. I noticed that many of the grown-ups that I liked changed their opinions overnight. Suddenly, there were fewer Social Democrats and little talk of politics at all. Even when I called for Ferdinand Sundays at the pub, the men now sang or played cards. Some of Ferdinand's cronies stopped showing up altogether. We went to visit those who had previously been Ferdinand's staunchest supporters. The Schulzes didn't even let us into their apartment. The Reindorfs invited us in but only Frau Reindorf sat with us. "He had something to do," she said, and gave me a big piece of cake.

Only Herr Schmidt, the butcher, still welcomed us. He was all for killing every one of the Nazis. His talk of justified executions made no sense to me, but it sickened Ferdinand. When we reported to Anna what he had said, she suggested that his profession had inured him to death. Although he didn't kill the animals whose flesh he sold, he had to cut them apart. Anna thought this a gruesome profession. As far as meat was concerned, she held on to the Jewish belief that meat should be soaked free of all blood, which left it as tough as shoe leather.

People like the Grotkes were suddenly in command. Mother was around more often, too. She felt she could no longer protect us, and was clearly agitated and worried. Now she wanted us to move to another neighborhood. She thought it would enhance our chances to live decently if we were not associated in any form whatsoever with this working-class section of Berlin. More agitated and irritable than ever, she contradicted everything Anna and Ferdinand said. She believed that the Nazis would manage to get even her new connections on their side and there would be no stopping the Germans from becoming the most powerful nation on the Earth. Didn't we – Ferdinand, Anna, and I – want to be part of this great change and share the glory? This was her refrain.

It was clear to me, though not to them, that I wanted to be like the other children, even though I was used to being "different." As the daughter of a divorced woman and as an American citizen with a head of thick black hair cut in a Buster Brown style, I was not surprised when "Jewish" was added to the list of attributes that made me different from other children. Being different meant being thought of by others in opposition to the prevailing tone and tenor of the times; it rendered one suspect. My mother, for her part, worshipped being different. To her, acting like the masses was to enshrine the mediocre, and mediocrity, in her book, was a virtual crime. To my grandfather "different" meant not wanting to fit into the group, fitting in being something he did not even aspire to. He was a Social Democrat, not a Nazi or a Communist, the two parties vying for his membership. Unperturbed, he held forth at his *Stammtisch* on Sunday mornings.

About this time the question of *Jungmädel* – Germany's official organization of "young girls" – came up. Many older girls who lived on our street became *Jungmädel*, since it was the preparatory organization that funneled its members into Association of *Deutscher Mäden* (the League of German Girls). I very much wanted to join and share in the fun. They went camping, sang some good songs, played a lot of games, and seemed to enjoy their time together. My friend Brigitte was already a *Jungmädel*.

An older girl, she had been handpicked by my mother to be my playmate, according to what criterion I know not. Possibly Brigitte became her favorite because the girl curtsied when we met her and her mother on a shopping trip.

On one such trip I was vastly embarrassed. Mother bought huge amounts of linens and other household items, always of the finest quality. My tall mother, wrapped in a plush coat with a large fur collar held tightly against her fashionably sparse chest suddenly acquired an accent while puffing on a cigarette in a long-stemmed holder. She became the elegant personification of all the shoppers who descended on the economically tottering Germany. On the trip in question, she bought enough to outfit more than one apartment, and she put to use her amazing bargaining skills. She never bought any new feather beds though, remarking to the merchant: "My huzbant doez not like to sweat in bed. He likes ze sauna." Somehow this always led to an invitation for dinner from the merchant. Everyone assumed that she was on a bargain hunting spree with her last dollars because the Mark was "low."

Brigitte and I always liked each other too and sometimes met in the afternoon to play. She was part of Mother's plan to prime me to enter a "better class of people." She reminded both Anna and Ferdinand of their obligation to educate me. Ferdinand asked again if she wanted to make a monkey or a circus performer out of me. I fervently hoped mother would choose circus performer as my station in life. From my perspective, that role definitely placed me in a "better class of people." I had seen with my own eyes how they curtsied at the end of a performance. But mother disabused me of the notion while letting me know I could play with Brigitte, who came from "an acceptable family." I don't know what made her family more acceptable, but I was glad of Brigitte's friendship.

I went with Bridgett to her next *Jungmädel* meeting without telling anyone, and was greeted with friendly handclasps and a cheerful *"Heil Hitler."* We sang *Horst Wessel Lied* together, a marching song devoted to a hero who had already bled to death for the *Führer*. I began to feel slightly uncomfortable and thrillingly traitorous, quite aware of my treachery. I felt adventurous and freed from my family's heavy demands. The young troop leader greeted me and asked where I came from. Accustomed to astonished facial expressions, raised eyebrows, and great interest when only my name was mentioned, I trumpeted "Weehawken, New Jersey" and the troop leader's face fell.

"You are welcome to stay today as our guest," he lectured, "because we National Socialists are friendly to all peoples of the world but, because you are a foreigner, you must bring your *Stammbaum* [a printed family tree proving Aryan ancestry] so we can ascertain that you are Aryan. After that, we will be able to admit you as an honorary member only."

I felt crushed, thinking that maybe he meant a real tree. I saw myself carting a huge apple tree or an oak and buckling under the weight. "How big does it have to be?" I asked. The troop leader frowned: "You must perfect your German. You say: 'How *long* is your *Stammbaum*, or how *far back* can you trace your ancestry.' If there are Jews in your family, you must have no more than one-eighth non-Aryan blood to avoid mongrelization." The other girls, including Brigitte, raised their hands in the Hitler salute and yelled, *"Heil Hitler."* Later, I thought of them as the Greek Chorus accompanying my drama. But, unlike the Greek Chorus accompanying my dramas, no deus ex machina appeared for me.

My adventure had even more far-reaching consequences. For once, Anna and my mother were horrified at me at the same time, though for different reasons. Anna was indignant that I could so easily forget that we were Jewish and Social Democrats. My mother was indignant that I wanted to join a bunch of ill-bred lower-class girls who would probably end up working in factories. The two of them carried on until I just turned my back and willed myself into the brooding silence my mother detested. I had discovered earlier in life that I could defend myself against their tirades by emotionally removing myself, sometimes to the point of not even hearing what was said. Oma Anna correctly surmised that I was either scared or "off in a world of her own." But Mother did not buy the explanation. "Stubborn, just plain stubborn. She is going to disgrace me with these boorish manners," she yelled.

While Hitler and his party tightened their grip on the population, there were furtive meetings in our apartment after I was sent to bed. I wasn't really sure who came and went late at night but I often heard speaking, sometimes in foreign languages. All were fleeing from something.

Now my mother changed her tune entirely and dismissed the Brownshirts and the whole Nazi ideology as irrelevant and tailor-made for the lower classes only. "One can only benefit from having them clean up the rabble," she declared imperiously. Anna wasn't willing to give in. "And what higher order do you belong to, my daughter?" she inquired. "Your father and I were farmers, plain and simple." "Not so plain and simple," my mother replied and reiterated for the millionth time: "If we were not Jewish, we would automatically have become members of the Junkers. The title went along with the land. That early Jakob must have been superior even though he was a Jew. You yourself told me about the *Freibrief* [the diploma providing the recipient with all the rights and privileges of a Prussian citizen, given to certain Jewish families by the government].

"But we *are* Jewish," Anna persisted. "And your superior ancestor was probably a horse thief who somehow conned his way into the good graces of the upper crust." "Why must you always play the plebeian?" my mother complained. "Walt [Mother's Gentile beau] doesn't say anything when you put on your 'last honest working man' routine, but his family would surely object if you carried on like this in front of them."

"If they are truly gentle folk they would have the good manners not to embarrass me," Anna retorted, now with amusement. "And why should it matter anyway? Or are you deluding yourself that your fine gentleman will actually marry you?"

As it turned out, Anna was wrong this time. Walt did marry my mother and it was Anna who started to drivel and show bad manners. She became increasingly morose when she saw that the people she valued either moved away, suddenly and without notice, or simply vanished. The Brownshirts were an ever-increasing presence in our lives. At first, there was excitement in the air when they came to take somebody. The children would form tight circles around the vans that transported prisoners. The women stopped their shopping and stayed to look on as well. There weren't many neighborhood men around anymore. They all had jobs by then, some were even among the guards, policemen, and Brownshirts who carted our neighbors and friends away. Soon, nobody paid any attention when yet another family disappeared.

I increasingly stopped trying to figure out what the grown-ups meant by their behavior. I ceased paying much attention to them and was content to play games with Helga, my closest friend. I liked school. I liked the safety of the rules and regulations and the way Herr Herbst, our teacher, clearly liked me, even though I was from the outside and could not join the Hitler Youth. I pondered at first exactly why he liked me, but then settled for the simple fact that he did. Grown-ups were so mysterious and powerful that I felt much younger than I was, more like the way I remembered feeling – at least so I thought – when I was a baby who had just come here from America and could not even speak German.

Another incident from about the same time comes back to me with astonishing clarity. Anna and I were just home from shopping. We had passed Grau's Coal and Wood Emporium. Herr Grau was a well-known and well-liked merchant who was married to a Jewish woman. She kept to her apartment and did not take part in the informal coffee drinking of the other women. Nor did Herr Grau belong to any political party. Still, it was known that he had been invited to divorce his wife and join the Nazi party in order to become one of their re-purified Aryans. He politely refused.

Such refusals were not well-tolerated. Slogans began to appear on his wooden fence: "Grau Grau, your wife is a Jewish sow" was one of the milder ones. He stoically repainted the fence each time. This afternoon, as Anna and I reached Grau's, we saw a seething mass of men battering at something, and not all of them were Brownshirts. We recognized some as people who lived on our block or on our street. Anna knew what was happening. She parked me and the groceries a short distance away and, straight as an arrow, marched into the murderously excited group. They looked like one giant animal to me, with many arms and fists and even more massive legs, a monstrous accumulation of lust for the kill, much like the giant in my fairy tale book who liked to dismember people who crossed his path. Anna was not deterred. "Stop that," she shouted. The monster broke up into identifiable individuals who looked around in astonishment at someone daring to interrupt their ritual. It was Herr Grau who they had been at work beating.

Anna pushed her way through the startled mob, helped him to his feet, and supported him as they made their way through the temporarily quieted throng. She motioned to me to bring our groceries while she held Herr Grau upright and managed to pull and push him up the stairs into our apartment. She put compresses on his many bruises and tended to several open wounds. "They used their knives on you," she stated angrily. "Anna, you saved my life," he answered weakly, "and you know they will get you for this. You are in danger yourself."

Anna sighed, "Ferdinand thinks we are safe because he is a Swiss. And who'll help all of the people we sluice through to the outside if we go away? Ferdinand thinks all the long-time members of the group have suddenly become old women. They are afraid they will end up in those labor camps. If it weren't for Charlotte's [my mother's] help, we couldn't manage altogether."

"Charlotte helps you? I can't believe it! I thought she had joined the Party, the way she carries on these days, with her fine gentleman friend and his ritzy car. Forgive me Anna, but it galls me to see that daughter of yours put on such airs, as though she weren't one of us. It's hard to believe that she is your daughter."

Anna's face became red. I couldn't tell if she was angry or hurt or both. "Well, she is my daughter, and I can't do anything about that now can I? She works in the foreign currency department of the bank. That's why she can help out. She helped Levandowski – remember the tailor? She got his money into Switzerland somehow. She's done as much and more for others she doesn't even know." This was the first time I had heard that my mother worked for a bank. I was proud of her for helping people with their money and instantly forgave her for accusing me of lying so often. My mother was a heroine! How wonderful! I couldn't wait to tell Helga.

Anna was not finished with Herr Grau. "You should have a doctor look at those deep cuts near your throat. They may not heal as quickly as the more superficial ones," she admonished as she packed up some pain-killing herbal mixture and disinfectant tea. But Grau had more to say. "You should think of the child," he warned. "What will become of her if anything happens to you?" "She is one of the reasons I am staying," Anna told him. Then Grau: "Her mother will make a Nazi out of her just to push herself up that social ladder of hers."

I thought Anna would spit on the floor like the old men in Sbrinkov, there was such venom in her voice. I wondered for the thousandth time if my mother was really Anna's daughter, like I was always told. It was another mystery, to be filed away along with other unsolvable, irreconcilable statements I had already stored up. Why did my mother have to help people with their money? Did she take some of it or was she like the ladies in the bank where Anna and I changed Ferdinand's pay check into Marks? They were exceedingly pleasant, I thought, always asking Anna how she was and if she wasn't overdoing it, taking such good care of me.

Why the ladies were so interested in my mother was another of those mysteries I could only partially solve. Mother was an appraiser of fine arts and objets d'art in the bank where she worked. The nice ladies there would love to have my mother's job, they confided to me, but lacked her social connections. What, I asked Anna, did they mean by "social connections"? She snorted like she always did when something displeased her. "It's part of your mother's plan to become a fine lady," she told me. "The bank tellers are afraid of her." "But why?" I insisted. Anna gave me a cryptic answer: "She probably pays them a commission if they find something good enough for her." She refused to answer any more questions no matter how often or how hard I tried to wrest more information from her.

I discussed the situation with my friend, Helga. She too had heard tales about my mother in her family's pub. Fraulein Gutenfeld liked nothing better than to gossip about my mother. "She's really got it in for your mother. You'd better tell her to stop using so much make-up. Gutenfeld says it's not normal to smear that stuff on her face. It's perverse, she says, and she says you'll probably take after your mother and be perverse and make believe you are an Aryan." There was also a story that my American father was not my father at all. One of my mother's Jewish lovers, a rich one, was given that honor. But that story I knew how to deal with. Anna had told me all about how babies were born, so I knew that a rich German Jew could not possibly be my father because I was born in America. Helga saw it differently. "If your father was a rich German Jew, then you would be a full-blooded Jew and not just a mongrel," she remarked thoughtfully.

I felt sick to my stomach. I knew that what Helga said fit together with what Anna said. I quizzed Oma Amanda too. The police had come after Anna fixed up Herr Grau, although neither of them had summoned them. I suspected Frau Grotke of denouncing Anna and Herr Grau but held my peace because the old cow still came frequently to visit, snooping away and eager for the coffee and cake that Anna generously provided and that she was too poor to purchase or bake herself. The police were stern. They poked around in Anna's herb baskets and unguent pots. They stuck their noses into each bottle of medicine and questioned why we made wine in the pantry. We admitted that, at the end of summer, we had borrowed a *Leiterwagen,* a small wooden wagon that held its contents in wooden slats on its sides that looked like ladders. We loaded it with purple and white grapes bought at an illegal farmer's market, the "Gypsies Plaza" not far from our apartment. We all knew the market flourished because the local chief of police was a farm boy himself and liked the fresh produce the small farmers and gypsies brought into town.

But when the police came and asked us why we had interfered with Herr Grau, Anna and I both played dumb. Yes, we helped Herr Grau because we knew him and he had hurt himself somehow. We didn't know how. I was amazed at how easy it was to lie. Besides, Anna was lying too so it had to be all right. But it wasn't. No one noticed when I began to confuse events and people. Berlin was rife with too many beatings and suicides and thefts for anybody to take to task the testimony of one hyper-vigilant child. Helga and I swore that we would never let the grown-ups in on our secrets.

We spied on our families, just like the Hitler Youth had exhorted us to do, but not to catch them in the midst of illicit or illegal acts. We had a different purpose: We wanted to keep our grown-ups alive and away from the police. This was not always easy. For instance, the police hung around for days after the Grau incident and made us repeat the same story over and over. They kept asking Anna if we were Jewish. She denied it. "My husband is a Swiss citizen, and my granddaughter was born in America," she kept saying. When the police finally left, they were replaced by Brownshirts who told us they did this kind of "work" on their own without getting paid for it, as a patriotic gesture to the Fatherland. Eventually they too grew tired and left.

My mother was around more often during those days and weeks. She made noises indicating that she had "connections." Anna sniffed and padded away each time Mother asserted herself. One of the police lieutenants visited us also. I heard from my listening post under the table that he was an art historian, interested in some paintings a Jewish customer of Mother's owned. At least I thought that was what I heard. When I asked about it, Mother slapped me hard across the mouth and told me to keep it shut. I knew better than to argue with my mother. She always won, even when, initially at least, other grown-ups in my world believed me.

Our apartment house was fairly old. Its attic and laundry rooms were constructed of wood, the massive roofs were held up by huge beams covered with slate. I knew every nook and cranny of the attic where each family had, in addition to its small cellar storage bin, a compartment enclosed by wooden slats. All these partitions were highly flammable. The Nazis extended their choke hold even there. Each family was instructed to keep buckets of sand and water in their compartments so that fires could be quickly and efficiently doused before reaching major proportions. Especially around Christmas time there were many fires caused by candles stuck on dry Christmas trees. So buckets of sand and water appeared in some hallways and foyers as well. Inspectors appeared to make sure the new rules were followed. Obviously, making new rules that had to be enforced was another way of creating jobs, though this did not occur to me until much later. I had a good time playing with the sand, sometimes spilling it or creating mud pies alongside of them. Anna, otherwise so mild, sharply forbade these games.

One day I recognized why. I found a handgun wrapped in oilcloth and some rags. I dirtied my pinafore before I reburied the gun in my favorite blue bucket. My heart beat so loudly I was sure Anna would hear it and scold me again. I never told anyone what I had found. When thinking of that gun I sometimes imagined that it foretold the changes that were about to come.

chapter two
BEYOND MY FRONT DOOR

After the police and the Brownshirts left, Anna, Helga, and I often saw someone following us. I thought it might be Pauli, a boy I had met at my other grandparents' vegetable patch. Because he lived right across the street from us, he became one of the few friends Helga and I had. Pauli belonged to the Hitler Youth. After an initially intense friendship he stayed away from Helga and me for a while, though every so often he reappeared and asked us to show him our bottoms, becoming very provoked when we wouldn't. He shouted that when we grew up he would see to it that we would never have a good Aryan husband. Helga, wheezing and with blue lips, hushed him. "Your father was a gypsy," my usually gentle friend hissed. "I know because Fraulein Gutenfeld told us." Pauli turned grey. "The bitch," he fumed, "she'll ruin my reputation with the squad." Helga and I thought our information must be right.

We had never seen Pauli so upset before. After that, he tried to get each of us alone. He grabbed me one day when I went to the cellar to bring upstairs some potatoes we stored there.

His fly was open, and I gathered I was supposed to be afraid of his limp little worm of a penis. When I wasn't, he whimpered: "Damn you, you Jewish pig. Why don't you listen? I listened when the squad leader did it to me." The squad he referred to was the local group of Brownshirts. I was intrigued and wanted to know what he had to listen to. When he told me, it didn't make any more sense than the beating of Herr Grau and the old Jew Isaac or the whispered conversations of Anna and her friend or my mother's periodic outbursts. What I did understand was that the world was a very dangerous place and that one had to learn to manipulate and lie in order to stay alive. I also understood that none of the grown-ups around me could be told of my inner discovery. I would have to keep my family alive by myself as well as I could.

I had the vague understanding that such thoughts were not usual for a child. Anna often said: "One does what one can and hopes for the best." Oma Anna knew so much and was so good to many people that I decided she must be right about almost everything, whereas my mother was wrong about just about everything. She was given to stating, "Your childhood is the best time of your life. Enjoy it and stop looking so fierce this instant." This made no sense to me whatsoever. Certainly, my friend Helga and I were having a hard time rather than the best time of our lives. Helga's father, Herr Musterweg, had lost his job at the municipal transportation agency because he had been the shop steward for the Social Democratic Union and refused to join the Nazi Party, the NSDAP (*Nationalsozialistische Deutsche Arbeiterpartei*). Now he sat around the pub he ran, dispiritedly drawing beer for the few steady customers and trying not to get into arguments with the Brownshirts when they appeared on weekends to make trouble. The pub belonged to Martin and Elvira Strembunch, his in-laws and Helga's maternal grandparents, both of whom were then in a nursing home.

Most of the time, Herr Musterweg sat in an old leather armchair, his pipe clenched in his teeth. A large German shepherd watched the store while he slept, and Helga and I either played board games or practiced roller skating while holding on to the billiard table in the back room. We were not allowed to roller skate without permission outside because Helga easily started to wheeze with asthma when other children called her father "a traitor to the Fatherland." Later, we did our homework there as well. We also learned to quickly gather up our paraphernalia and scamper out of the back door, up the stairs to the Musterweg's apartment, when the Brownshirts appeared to get free beer and taunt the proprietor.

My mother soon heard about these incidents and decided that Helga was not a fit companion for me. The verdict was: "no more best friend Helga." I was forbidden to see Helga "so often," which in reality meant not at all. Oma Anna too had difficulties with this dictum from my mother, but when she tried to talk to Herr Musterweg about it, he bluntly told her that he did not approve of me either. I was not surprised. Only Opa Ferdinand remained unperturbed. He held forth at his *Stammtisch* on Sunday mornings, where the men drank their beer and argued about how to be manly, staying away from home until the last possible minute when their wives called them to come eat the gigantic meals they had prepared.

I noted that only the politically active "friends" of Opa Ferdinand's *Stammtisch* continued to show up for meetings. None of the professional agitators appeared any longer. Two or three of them had asked me to call them "Uncle," but at Anna's request, I stopped doing so. Oma thought they had shown too great an interest in having me sit on their laps as though I were very little. The games always ended with me upside down with my underpants exposed. I didn't really mind, savoring the attention.

As I mentioned, all was not going well with the small remnant of Social Democratic *Stammtisch*. The men came home later and later. Ferdinand blamed his own tardiness on his cronies. Various wives began to develop strategies to persuade their men to come home on time. For instance, Frau Oberndorf used the phone, still a rarely used instrument, to summon her Otto home. Otto was startled and resented the dime it cost to make to call. Why, he could have had another beer for that coin! Frau Schmitt came in person, jocularly threatening to wrap Herr Schmitt up in Nazi flyers (printed with the running ink). Anna had a more suitable method. She sent me to fetch Ferdinand, knowing that he found it hard to say "no" to me. I loved the assignment, especially because Anna, usually so practical, suggested that for these outings I should wear my Sunday dress. Some of the girls on the street had been in awe when I first wore my sky blue organdy dress and two of the boys had thrown mud at me. Pauli said it was because I looked so "chic."

So off I went, fervently hoping I would be successful in my mission. As soon as I appeared in the saloon, I knew something was not right. Mr. Schöneman, the pub owner, poured me a raspberry soda. How, I wondered, did he know this was my favorite? Ferdinand stumbled out of the men's room, took one look at me and lurched toward me. "Easy," several of the men standing at the high round drinking tables whispered amid futile gestures towards him. It was clear that they were trying to hide from me that my beloved and revered Social Democratic grandfather was totally soused. I drank my raspberry soda and tried to put authority into my voice, as I had heard Frau Musterweg do when someone in her pub became unruly.

Ferdinand laughed, coughed, picked me up under the arms and seated me on the bar. The metal, perforated to let spilled liquids find its way into the plumbing, was both cold and wet. I tried to squirm away, but Ferdinand forced me to stay there. "Huh?" he said to his buddies. "Didn't I tell you she is special? Nobody has a little girl like her." He suddenly let go of me and sped toward the men's room. This time I followed him. He was urinating. The full stream fascinated me and his genital seemed gigantic compared to the little thing Pauli had shown us.

On the way home he began to sing something about *Röslein, Röslein rot, Röslein auf der Heide* (Little Red Rose on the Heath). I didn't know whether to be embarrassed or to ignore his weird behavior. When we arrived home, Anna flew into a rage. "You promised me never to do that again!" she shouted. "And in front of the child, too. I never would have sent her for you if I had known you had fallen off the wagon. Charlotte will have a fit. And didn't I tell you, you can drink all you want at home? It's a disgrace to hide behind your so-called political convictions and then drink yourself into a stupor. Into bed with you now!"

I was more embarrassed by Anna's tirade than by Ferdinand's overindulgence. He seemed to have such a peachy, comfortable time and was pleased to see me, whereas Anna acted like an old witch. I only went to retrieve Ferdinand one further time and then it was without Anna's knowledge. I knew he was busy disgracing himself, so I went for him before Anna noticed he was late. He was so looped that he asked me to hold his penis while he dried it with paper. Although I thought Anna knew nothing of this, from then on the *Stammtisch* was held in our living room.

Despite all the people who came to see us for various reasons, Anna's closest friends, like Mother Gräfchen and Mathias auf der Heyde, never came to the meetings. Helga and Pauli made up for that. Pauli now came whenever he could get away from his "duties," as he referred to his voluntary attendance at the local branch of the Nazi party, where he ran errands of all sorts and was a kind of mascot. Oma Anna thought this indecent and threatened to tell Pauli's mother though none of us had ever met her. An aunt looked after him but did not see to it that he had clean clothes or warm boots in winter. We did not talk about what Pauli did at the Nazi's hangout, as we did not want Anna to hear anything about Pauli's "duties." Helga and I felt that he would eventually outgrow some of his strange (to us) behavior. We placed whatever it was he did with his penis on the same level as

Helga's asthma: something for which nobody was to blame and that would pass with time.

One reason we liked Pauli was that he let us know ahead of time when there would be a brawl. Apparently, the Brownshirts staged with great care their attacks on citizens who did not share their point of view. That way, they could claim their nasty jeering and brutal beatings were nothing but aggrieved racial purity. We did not know exactly what "racial purity" was, but we three knew we didn't have it. For one thing, you had to be blond and tall and have long braids to wind around your head. Helga and I felt totally outclassed. She had brown hair whereas Pauli and I had even less fashionable black hair. He tried to have his dyed once but was caught at the barber's by one of the Brownshirts who promptly took him to the party headquarters and gave him a good beating for his "unmanly behavior."

Pauli did not want our sympathy but continued to give us information that we passed on to our families. These protective gestures sometimes earned us an impatient "get out of here" from Helga's father, who was beginning to be even more depressed because the big front window of the pub had been broken three times, and he could no longer get insurance. Afterwards, he felt badly that he had spoken harshly to us and gave us one of the dried out chocolate bars he had for sale in the glass case that stood right in the middle of the narrow strip of sun that reached the wet bar. He had nurtured high hopes for his mini-confectionary, but the Brownshirts goaded him, saying he was acting like a Jew, turning a profit by selling goods at a higher price than he himself had to pay. Herr Musterweg feared for his family and for himself. So he let the chocolate melt and then dry and sold it half price. When the Brownshirts came, and Helga had managed to warn him beforehand, he managed to be jovial and did not respond to their taunts. But at other times that defense was beyond his endurance. He spat on the floor in front of them, forbade them to come into the pub, and had to be subdued by his apologetic wife.

Helga's mother was a little woman with withered hands

and a face that never let go of its apologetic expression, as if she were sorry to have been born. She thought of Helga as the most marvelous daughter a woman could have. I envied Helga because my mother was on my back constantly about my many failings. I was actually glad that she wasn't home much. I made believe that Anna was my mother and that worked out just fine, even though most of her friends still felt I was too much for her, especially because "the times were changing."

For me, that meant I was approaching school age. I knew that I would have to leave the protective island Anna had built for me and my friends, but I was also eager for new adventures. Helga was sure we would get into a lot of trouble because we had already been told that "we stuck our noses where children had no business." I noted the admonition and checked it against my experiences. Should children really not stick their noses into certain places? Together with Pauli we had kept the front window of the pub from getting smashed even more often and had saved Herr Musterweg from additional beatings by the Nazis. Pauli said he would surely "get it" if he didn't watch out. Herr Musterweg must have been on our side anyway because he allowed Helga and me to play together, my mother's directive notwithstanding. I concluded that grown-ups had the luxury of several sets of opinions and behaviors among which they could switch at will while children had a single duty: To obey and be good.

My grandmother often left me with Mother Gräfchen when she could not take me with her to a meeting or visit. My mother had made inquiries about her and now found her totally unsuitable as babysitter. Rumors swelled around her. According to the local Protestant clergyman, Reverend Abortus, Mother Gräfchen was one of the declared enemies of the Aryan race. Some people, like Frau Grotke, thought that Mother Gräfchen had been in the employ of a fine lady but had been fired because she had stolen jewelry. Others agreed that she had been employed by a fine lady and had gone off to Africa with her mistress to minister to the heathens. Yet another version had it that Mother Gräfchen herself had been a missionary doctor and, having been held hostage by guerillas, was so upset by the capture that she returned to Germany.

I absolutely adored her darkened apartment, full of cats, with oriental screens that hid corners and gave her large rooms the atmosphere of geodesic temples. Heavy velvet and brocade curtains full of dust smelled of perfume once dried on the tight bodices of Mother Gräfchen's long-dead family and friends. Oma Anna and I kept it secret that Mother Gräfchen was our preferred baby sitter. She showed me pictures of beautiful ladies, many of them pierced by arrows or in the process of being eaten by unlikely monsters. These were called "saints." Some of these ladies rolled their eyes heavenward and clutched themselves in the vicinity of their crotches, signs of belonging to the subcategory of "virgin saints." My mother had warned me to leave my crotch alone, so I was puzzled by this display of touching forbidden body parts by such prominent grown-ups.

Another category of ladies altogether were those in fabulous gowns with full skirts or bustles and lot of curls and jewelry. Much to my delight, Mother Gräfchen had clothes of that type for me to play dress-up with. I did not mind the mewing cats and their attendant odors, but when Mother Gräfchen took off the gown she had been modeling for me, I found I greatly disliked her odor, which settled like a swarm of flying ants in my nostrils. She had been demonstrating how to dance a quadrille, which required me to pass under her arms repeatedly. Dancing with her was bad enough but when she removed the red and gold ball gown, her body odor destroyed my pleasure in our games. I protested that I did not want to stay with her any longer.

Never at a loss for provocative action – she gave the tight-fisted Communist salute when the Nazis marched by – Mother Gräfchen took me to her Roman Catholic Church. I loved the place, being much taken with the plaster saints with their stiff-gilded halos and smell of incense. My family didn't want me to go there because I had once hidden in a confessional until Oma Anna, at her wits' end, called my Opa Ferdinand home from work to help look for me. On this day, a special ceremony was taking place. Basking in the pleasant awe I usually felt in that sacred place, I noticed many children standing in a tight row lining red velvet carpals. "Look," I shouted. "Just like in your place."

Mother Gräfchen firmly placed her hand across my mouth and dragged me toward the children. Her hands smelled of onions, wet earth, and mothballs. I tried to bite her, but all the children suddenly knelt down. I remained standing even though Mother Gräfchen had also doubled up on the floor. A beautiful golden figure appeared in my line of vision. I had never seen anyone so splendid anywhere, not even among Mother Gräfchen's pictures. I rushed through the kneelers, pushing them aside like so much mown hay. The golden figure came closer and smiled at me. Even his shoes were golden. He stopped in front of me, smiled deeply into my eyes and asked benignly: "And are you a true believer, my child?" I could hardly bear the joy, the pleasure of being spoken to by this heavenly, crowned person. I nearly wet myself. But I had to tell him the truth so he would love me forever. "No," I said. "I am half and half." I was in trouble, all right!

Reverend Abortus looked after the Protestant people in the area and presided over a small brick church. He was very proud of having received a post in Berlin and tried to make friends with Anna. He seemed to be both attracted and repelled by her. He, too, visited in order to benefit from Anna's famous baking and also to speak with deep conviction about the heavenly advantages of belonging to his particular denomination. I did not trust him because when he stroked my hair he did it so rapidly and hard that it hurt. It helped me understand what the phrase "with a heavy hand" meant, as Hitler frequently used the term to describe how the German people had suffered indignities under the heavy hand of foreigners and non-Aryans. The Reverend Abortus also had views on nationality and race that he shared with his hostess. Although God's son had no known nationality, he intoned, historians might someday discover that he was an Aryan.

The Herr Reverend voiced his dismay over the religious lethargy of his flock and discussed it with Anna. Many of the older people had turned away from their churches, going back to folk customs long abandoned. The old Edda – a collection of Norse poems from the 13th century – with its cruel multiple gods, Wotan, Freya, and Loki, was becoming vogue in the Nazi Party. I ate it all up under the tablecloth along with the *Sandkuchen* (pound cake). Helga found a book of those tales on her father's shelf and we pored over it together, as I had taught myself to read German at an early age.

So many things seemed to change around us. For instance, Helga and I had been taught to look for a policeman if we ever were lost or got into trouble. We understood about the "trouble" part but not about the being "lost." We were always with our adult, so how could we get lost? And we persisted in believing that the job of policemen was to protect us.

I changed my mind soon after an incident that took place just after I entered public school. Coming home from kindergarten, on the corner of Beuel Strasse and Hohenstaufen Strasse in Berlin, I saw a bunch of Brownshirts busy beating up an old man. They were silent, beating with great efficiency. One could only hear the tortured breath and occasional scream of the old man. I was fascinated and edged as close as I dared. The old man saw me and with a bloody mouth and broken hand made me understand that I was to run away, run away fast. But I stood frozen watching them beat him until he was a broken bundle of rust-colored clothes on the pavement. Then I ran to where I knew a policeman was directing traffic. He came with me right away, but when he saw the rusty clothes bundle, he kicked it with his foot and said, "It's only old Isaac, the fishmonger. A Jew and troublemaker. Go home, little girl. We will protect you from the likes of that."

I don't know if there was still life in Isaac the Jew. Perhaps he died because I did not help him, because I ran home and didn't tell anyone what I had seen. Usually my best friend Helga was with me, but that day she had missed school because of her asthma. Nor did I tell Oma Anna about what I had seen either, although she knew something was wrong and questioned me, wheezing herself into a frenzy when I would not admit to harboring secrets. Eventually I became convinced that the Isaac incident was a nightmare or just a daydream.

Occasionally I made up a fantasy that my father had written me a letter and then my mother screamed at me for lying and ruining her chances to enter the circle of fine people she longed to be part of. She remain agitated and overexcited during her occasional visits. To calm her down I tried extra hard to use the right utensil while eating, shuddered suitably when Oma Anna served fish with meat knives, and even told Opa Ferdinand that he had better drink his beer out of a glass instead of out of a bottle. He was so startled by my curt request that he got up and took a glass and proceeded to teach me how to pour beer without too much foam on top. "That's how the Musterwegs keep the devil from the door," he explained. "When filling a glass you can make it half full with foam and make a few extra pennies that way. The customer gets half of what he paid for and the barkeep earns a bit more. Only God knows how they keep body and soul together over there."

Indeed, business was going from bad to worse at the pub. But old Frau Musterweg had built up a fairly decent clientele, not by catering to the drinkers or to the few customers who ordered something for lunch, but by cooking daily for a bunch of resident "bachelors." These were often men who were *herunter gekommen* (down on their luck). They were so poor and earned so little that they could not afford a room of their own, but paid a pittance to another poor family to sleep in their kitchen after the family had retired. Pauli's aunt had one of them in her kitchen and another one at the end of their long, narrow hallway. They had to keep their timing impeccably correct so as not to interfere with each other. Old Frau Musterweg earned her own meals by cooking for others. Looking at our grown-ups' lives, Helga and I became convinced that they had no idea of what was going on. They seemed not to see how much was changing. Some families, including the Grotkes, had acquired motorcycles with little sidecars attached to them. Herr Richfield even gave all the kids a ride, every kid but me, that is. Helga explained that it was because I was Jewish, not that my Jewishness meant anything to her. When her turn came, she took the ride anyway.

The *Reichsdeutschen* were streaming into Germany at that time. They were folk whose people had left the Fatherland generations ago to live in all parts of the world but had retained their German heritage. Hitler had invited them back to Germany to strengthen the Aryan race. At the same time, he continued to plead for more *Lebensraum*, for more land for Aryans to spread out and live. I noticed the discrepancy right away, but my mother told me to keep quiet.

Helga and I kept more and more to ourselves, though sometimes we were joined by Pauli. Mainly we talked about my being an American and the fact that we both wanted to be like Anna, who came from Silesia. Among the many people who knocked on her door, those who came from that region always received the biggest sandwich or piece of cake. It seemed to matter a great deal to her where one came from. She liked *Landsleute*, the people from her own region. I did not enjoy the privilege of having someone with whom I could identify. How nice, I thought, if my father and the Americans would gather me in.

chapter three
THE UNRAVELING

Oma Anna counseled me not to talk to anyone about my place of birth because of the "times." My mother had me totally confused. She accused me of lying when I was completely convinced of my veracity. She used to stand in front of me, shake her head and sigh, "She is a total pagan. She is going to disgrace me with the Udebeks." On another occasion, she told me I better behave when I met my new grandmother. A new grandmother? I had two already! Helga figured it out: "She is going to marry her boyfriend," she sagely nodded. I screamed: "She can't do that. She is married to my father in America."

We had discussed the situation in the main room of the pub where Fraulein Gutenfeld had apparently overheard us. Rumors flew around like butterflies looking for a place to put their eggs. By the time my mother became aware that once again the neighborhood was discussing her affairs, it was rumored that she was a bigamist, and that she was trying to get rid of me because I was the stumbling block holding up her forthcoming marriage to a high-ranking Nazi official. It had never occurred to me that we might need shielding or that we might be taken away in a truck like some of our neighbors had been. Helga and I had questioned our adults and were either slapped or forbidden to talk about such things. My mother was outraged that I should be thinking and talking "dirty"; she accused me of lying and pulled my hair.

Anna and I went down to Miss Natalie Ingelweier's flat to pay the rent. I liked going there as, usually, I was the only child. The two ladies would settle down to a cup of tea and *trockenen Kuchen* (cake without icing). They gossiped about neighborhood matters and sometimes about political issues. For instance, they speculated why someone called the Rotte Lotte had drowned herself in the *Landwehrkanal*, the canal that ran through the middle of Berlin. Oma Anna was quite certain it was because of her communist activities, which led to an order for her arrest. Although they almost never hid the topics of their conversation from me, in this case they lowered their voices so that I could barely hear. Rotte Lotte, I learned, had been in a Nazi prison previously and could not face another incarceration. By now we knew of many people who had been arrested. Some came back thin and grey and didn't talk to anyone. Others did not come back at all.

Oma Anna and Miss Ingelweier were not the only ones who dared to whisper of the prisons. Anna was glad to hear that Miss Ingleweier too found Herr Grotke unbearable since his appointment as SA warden for our block. In this capacity, he was entitled, even forced, to spy on his neighbors, to write down their political opinions and how much money they contributed to *Winterhilfe* (the annual winter collection of food and money for the poor), and to observe more generally how they fit into the New Order.

A new directive made Miss Ingelweier very angry. When she went to register for her contribution to *Winterhilfe*, Grotke told her that from now on her name would include "Sarah."

Anna took the younger woman's hand in hers. "We all are Sarah now," she gently said. But Miss Ingelweier would not be mollified: "How dare they. I am Natalie and always will be. I should have gone with my brothers and sisters." This elegant lady, of whom I was sometimes afraid, now needed Oma Anna as much as I did. Perhaps she was even as scared as I was. And yet, we had always thought of the Ingelweiers as powerful because, after all, they owned the entire apartment house and were very rich.

There used to be many Ingleweiers. There was always happy noise and the smell of fresh baking around their apartments, which took up a whole floor of the building. They loved living in the old place, and the income from the rents allowed them to attend Berlin University. But since the old parents died, the younger group moved away. Natalie, the oldest sister, old maid that she was, wanted to stay, to take care of her parents' grave and preserve the apartment house for her brothers and sisters. Perhaps she had a premonition or heard rumors that soon Jews would not be allowed to own such properties. I asked Anna why Miss Natalie had to preserve anything, and why the rest of her family had gone away. After all, they owned the house and were rich. Why did they have to leave? Was it the same reason that kept my real father in America?

Anna sighed and shook her head. "No," she answered with another sigh. "It is the times. The Nazis don't want them here, but Natalie thinks that they will not harm her because she is an 'old maid.'" I didn't understand why old maids should be any different than other women, nor did I understand what "time" had to do with the Nazis. I had heard on the radio that they would build an empire that would last one thousand years and had seen my grandfather sneer in response. This "time," I thought, must be a curious substance.

Time seemed to stretch forever the day we went to pay our rent that month. We went into Natalie's apartment. The door stood open, which did not surprise us. She always left the door open when she expected people to come to pay their rents. But it was quiet, very quiet in the apartment. We went through the red plush living room into the small hall that led to the office where we knew we should find Miss Natalie with her receipt book.

We puzzled at the open door to the kitchen, listening to the silence. Anna must have sensed something because she stiffened and grabbed for my hand. We went into the kitchen. Miss Natalie seemed to be leaning against the window with the two large panes opening like a door. Anna gasped. She covered my head with her shawl and pushed me back into the hall. But I had already seen that Miss Natalie was not standing by herself. She had wrapped a stout belt around her neck and fastened it to the place where the two cross beams of the window met. She must have stood and hung there for some time because there was a strange smell, as if some sick people had camped out there. Anna ran to the living room dragging me with her. She dialed and then hung up before anyone could answer. "Come," she said. "We don't want to call attention to ourselves." I understood that this was why nobody was there, why our noisy and nosy neighbors were not clamoring and exclaiming about Miss Natalie. They did not want to call attention to themselves either. I knew they were all sighing and saying: "In these times, you never know…"

That afternoon Grotke, in his uniform, nailed a big placard on the new bulletin board in the hall. It announced that all real estate owned by Jews would be confiscated and returned to its rightful owner, the German people. Those Jews who were loyal to Germany were generously permitted to stay and run the properties for their new masters, who would be appointed by the state. Oma turned pale. This new humiliation gave her one of the fierce headaches that had begun to plague her. She tried her own herbal potions, but to no avail. She could not understand how suddenly people had become so uncaring and shut off from each other. "We had a moral prerogative once," she muttered. "Where is all that glory of the soul?" While I tried to look up what "prerogative" meant, Mother Gräfchen came over and took care of her. Then she sent me out to find Helga and Pauli. She cautioned us not to say anything to anybody and to stay in the apartment, not to go out under any circumstances. She thought the pub especially would be a dangerous place for us. Anna begged her not to endanger herself when making funeral arrangements. She sneered and took off. We children never found out what sort of funeral Miss Natalie had. But we did find out what "sitting shiva" meant. Oma Anna, Oma Amanda, and Mother Gräfchen sat and mourned Miss Natalie for the prescribed time. Nobody came to offer condolences or to speak of the deceased. After all, she was a suicide, and a Jewish suicide at that.

In the absence of any relatives, the apartment house automatically became the property of the state. We would have to pay our rent to some office and were admonished to give Herr Grotke a few Marks each month to let Oma Anna continue her work with the women who came to her. He granted her what he called an *Arbeitsberechtigung* (an official right to work).

While the friends did their mourning, Helga, Pauli, and I started to think about what would happen to Miss Natalie. I was inclined to go along with the Christian notion Helga tried to teach me, despite my initial dislike of Heaven as a good place to end up. It seemed nice and safe to be good like Helga, and then to go to Heaven rather than to be bad like . . . I wasn't sure I knew anyone bad enough to qualify for Hell. I didn't hold on to that belief too long, but at the time it suited me to think of Miss Natalie as an angel, not a standing corpse turning weird colors. We scared ourselves talking about death, especially since the grown-ups were so wrapped up in their own grief. Oma Anna even forgot to bake a cake. She said that if these were normal times, all the neighbors, especially the Jewish ones, would have come with enough food to feed an army, so that the bereaved would not have to lift a finger.

We decided to go to the Jewish cemetery to investigate and find out what we could. An old man was always there, clad in black with a broad brimmed hat holding down his long white hair and a beard streaming down his broad chest. He mumbled prayers for the dead whose relatives had become so estranged from their Hebrew heritage that they could not say blessings and prayers themselves, and made a meager living from the few pennies he received for his services. During better times, he was well-fed because pious housewives invited him for meals. It was said that he had been a learned and holy rabbi long ago in Russia, but after he saw his family slaughtered in front of him during a pogrom, he became mad and fled on foot all the way to Berlin. Opa Ferdinand used to say, only half-jokingly, "The only mad thing he did was come to Germany."

My mother and Helga's parents were livid when they found out that we had gone to the cemetery. Mother especially was sure the *Gestapo* (the secret police) would investigate why children were involved. "Do you realize that the state can take the child from us? You know I haven't been able to get legal custody of her because that failure of a husband in New York won't give me a divorce." Oma Anna just shook her head. The police did arrive but didn't do anything but politely inquire if we knew of any reason why the poor lady had done away with herself. They soon left, but not before accepting a cup of coffee from Anna.

chapter four
LIVES TRANSFORMED

Before Miss Natalie's death, Helga, Pauli and I had talked about how silly some grown-ups were, how others frightened us, and how we would make everything so much better once we were no longer children. It was just a question of time until we could fix things and be the adults. But the death of someone we knew so well, someone who had died because she wanted to – we could hardly believe it. We had been taught that grown-ups could control their lives. When some clearly could not do so, we could only ask: Why? We took care not to ask *our* grown-ups. It would have been too frightening to find out that they too belonged to the powerless group.

We could not explain why some of our neighbors disappeared, but assumed they were moving somewhere else. Miss Natalie had often told Anna and me that she had to ask some people to leave because they could not afford the rent. She was always upset when this happened and conferred with Anna about where she could send the unfortunates. Pauli, Helga, and I deduced from these tales of poverty and distress that some people were simply unlucky. "They were unfortunate," as Anna said. We therefore thought of them not as powerless but as "the Unfortunates." By this time, we were convinced that being a child was, somehow, a punishment for something we had done without realizing it, and we were thus condemned to being powerless. So how could one become a powerful adult? Although we had evidence that women had babies who first became children and later adults, the actions of many people we knew somehow seemed "not grown up" to us. So we waited and watched, looking for answers. Often we were the only ones present when the Unfortunates were forced to move on. Oma Anna brought cake or sandwiches and coffee, and Mother Gräfchen came to say "good-bye and God bless" and then crossed herself. I knew by then that she was not writing or drawing on air but performing a religious rite.

Helga, Pauli, and I felt sad when we saw the accumulation of households on the sidewalk, waiting for whatever movers were available. The swarm of rowdy kids who usually gathered at neighborhood happenings did not materialize. We became tense when a tax collector from the city of Berlin occasionally appeared and put a tax claim stamp on a sofa that perhaps still held, within its whimpering springs, the crater that some grandmother's body had created when she could no longer walk and had to spend many hours there.

We knew the Briefenreiters slightly, having gone to school with their oldest daughter. Our stomachs churned when we saw our classmate carrying her grandmother's shoes because the old lady's feet were so swollen that they no longer fit. Sitting in a kitchen chair, her son and daughter-in-law had carried her down three stories. Another time, the tax collector put his stamp on a dining room table, which had once graced the rooms of a fallen family. It was warped now, having had to do service as a kitchen table. No one but the tax collector would have found it valuable. But much as we hated these departures, their impact paled alongside the sight of Jewish families loaded on trucks already stuffed with their furniture or driven down the middle of the street like a herd of frightened animals.

At first the neighborhood women tried to help, arguing with the soldiers or policemen. Frau Musterweg even offered them free beer (but to no avail), and Helga was proud of her mother for the first time. But when a soldier knocked down Frau Grotke with the blunt end of his rifle, everyone became frightened. After all, Herr Grotke had become a *Grosses Tier,* a Big Shot, in the Nazi party – and still his wife was attacked? Nobody said anything at all after that. The women made believe they didn't see or hear anything, ever. Helga, Pauli, and I hid behind the huge wooden doors that were large enough to let a coach and four horses into the yard. The apartment house had been built long ago for people who could afford to have such luxuries. But the house, like many of its inhabitants, had become "unfortunate." For a long time the yard was merely empty, holding nothing but the garbage cans. Now, there were some of those funny motorcycles with sidecars and many bicycles chained to the walls. When Anna and I looked out of the kitchen window, we could tell who was home and who was not by which conveyances were in the yard.

When Jewish neighbors were "resettled," as Anna read to us from the papers, Helga, Pauli, and I tried not to cry because we had been taught in school that German youth must be stalwart and strong. We agreed, but wanted to use our stalwartness and strength to save our own families who, in our opinion, had not the slightest idea of the danger they were in. So how could one become grown-up, stalwart, and strong in the shortest possible time?

The bunch of children who used to play amicably together now taunted one another unmercifully. Many practiced being Brownshirts and quite seriously inquired into each other's genealogy. Sometimes an unknown grown-up would stand and watch us. Others shook their heads and walked away.

One openly cried and then gave us all candy. The mothers told all the little girls not to talk to strangers.

One day, in the Musterweg's pub, Fraulein Gutenfeld announced that "*der Führer* was routing out all the criminal elements," throwing meaningful glances at Helga's father and then at me. He ignored her but others did not. The impoverished bachelors stopped coming; they made enough money now to rent whole rooms. Mainly they appeared to get jobs in new factories that made mysterious metal parts or on the crews that poured concrete and did all those things road workers do. These workplaces were created by the government and reeked of the Nazi touch; workers were enjoined in "patriotic" songfests and were expected to contribute to the Nazi party. They also provided hot meals to employees for very little money. So old Frau Musterweg lost an important source of income, and Helga did not get new clothes for school and clung even more to Oma Anna and me.

Oma Anna seemed preoccupied. She was as kind to us as ever, made us sweet puddings, and had us help put up her herbal ointments and drops, but she never sang any more. I was now too big to sit under the table, but I did not mind because Oma Anna allowed Helga and me to attend her women's meetings. My mother objected strenuously, but Anna said: "What makes you think the children do not know what is going on? Let them hear from our side as well." Her ladies' coffee and cake sessions now focused more on what was happening in the streets than on unwanted pregnancies and terrible tales of bad marriages. The women seemed to get beaten up just as often but not by their own husbands. Now they were beaten by neighborhood bullies who took over and tried to force them to join the Nazi establishment. There were now soup kitchens and dormitories for single women, and these places needed help of all sorts, cooks and maids and chaperones. And all "establishment" employees received medical insurance and old-age pensions better than those put in place in the late nineteenth century by Bismarck.

"No more prostitutes," billboards shrieked at the world. There were rumors, however, that good blond women could go to certain places and when their health checked out okay, they would be admitted to something called the *Lebensborn* (spring of life). Here, they were free to mate with an Aryan man of their choice. The resulting pure Aryans would be brought up in state run boarding schools without parents. Permanent relationships among the progenitors were discouraged. The children of their fleeting unions belonged to the State and were to grow up totally unencumbered by emotional ties to a family. Helga and I wondered about this while listening to Oma's friends munching *Berliners* (jelly donuts) or apple cake, fresh out of Anna's coal stove.

It all sounded totally implausible to us. How could a child have no parents? Even Pauli had a mother someplace. We began to wonder where and who his father was. No one had ever alluded to him. At least I knew mine was in America, and I began to wish I could go to live with him. America seemed to have everything I wanted: Lots of books, high schools with interesting electives, no stiff table manners, and a lot of kids who had more freedom to misbehave than any of us ever dreamed of. We gleaned this information from the newspapers Helga's father ordered for his few remaining customers. During weeks when trade was particularly slow he went to the tram station on the corner and fished out from the trash baskets the newspapers left there by wealthier people on their way to work. Mrs. Musterweg sometimes ran a lukewarm iron across pages that were too badly wrinkled. We children felt we needed all the information we could get because our families seemed so oblivious to all the changes around us.

I had a sense that something truly groundbreaking was going to happen in my own life. Mother was home even less, supposedly in the pursuit of her job. She now wore even more wonderful clothes and was often picked up for a date by her suitor, Walt von Udebek. He was clearly a gentleman and openly voiced his disapproval of the Nazis. This should have endeared him to Opa Ferdinand, but instead Ferdinand sneered at his manicured nails when he kissed Anna's hand. He appeared in a silver grey Mercedes and had his own chauffeur. The latter, Herr Schloske, sat like a statue when the street kids clustered around the car. In desperation, he asked if he might take the children for a ride. He hated being called a plutocrat and a bloodsucker and besides, he feared the car would get scratched up by the "heathens." So while Walt and my mother were visiting Anna, Schloske drove car loads of laughing, screaming street kids around the block. It was far from common to own one's car back then, let alone to employ a driver. I would soon come to enjoy the privileges of wealth, but before my own life changed, everyday experiences drove me even deeper into myself.

chapter five
A MISFIT

For a long time I felt that it was right to be half and half, meaning half Jewish and half Lutheran. That way, I could claim to belong to two groups at one time and adapt my behavior accordingly. That the Jewish side prevailed so often had little to do with my own volition. Hitler and his brutes made sure of it for me. How could anyone, even a little girl, choose the Nazis to be her ideal? Apparently many children viewed the situation differently than Helga and me. Some seemed to stagger like their fathers after drinking too much beer. The idea that they could "tell on their parents" made them drunk with power. This kind of magic power could only be earned at the expense of another, and many children were eager to gain what they did not deserve.

Too much reading was discouraged by many parents. They wanted good, strong sons who would do their bidding and obedient daughters who kept their mouths shut and married early, all for the glory of the Fatherland. Many fathers had participated in the First World War and the ensuing political revolution. Helga and I listened to their stories in the pub when they let everyone know that discipline was all that was needed to straighten out their unruly families. They might not agree with Hitler but their women had to toe the line laid down by them, or else! Women like my mother, who reached for a life above their station, were viewed with disdain.

Within the Nazi party there were some influential women, of course. We children saw their virtues advertised everywhere. One had to be blond, wear the ethnic dirndl when not in uniform and have long hair, which could be wound around one's head, constituting one's "womanly glory." Helga and I managed conformity only with respect to hair length, as we both had long braids hanging down on either side of our faces, but the rest was totally beyond our abilities. We at once gave up the idea of trying. Further, we both liked to read, which in itself disqualified us from being viewed as the true future of German womanhood. When we first learned of the encouragement to inform on one's parents, we thought somebody must have misunderstood. For instance, Helga pointed out that my mother, with her fine dresses and good perfume and uppity male friend was a less than ideal German mother. But what could one report about her, given that we weren't even Nazis. That she used lipstick? And what exactly was so unpatriotic about lipstick?

Anyway, our peers did not share our doubts. They saw knights in shining armor or saints come to glorify the German race where I saw demons and monsters. The old Germanic myths corroborated my concerns. They spoke of dwarfish blacksmiths who manufactured invincible swords and gave them to the evil ones for their own selfish ends. The same trolls, in various disguises, showed up again in the operas Opa Ferdinand liked to listen to on his wind-up Victrola. I preferred the bel canto of Italian opera at that early age. That German guy, Wagner, with his dragon Fafnir who guarded the gold which didn't seem to belong to him, and the thundering herds of females devoted solely to their father, Wotan – and wasn't it forbidden just to love your father? – all gave me strange feelings. I wanted to run away from the Valkyries, even if Opa liked to listen to their hoofs clattering through the clouds. This had to be a trick, I thought, because how could you make such noise in the clouds, when I knew for a scientific fact that thunder only happened under certain atmospheric conditions, as my grandfather had painstakingly explained to me when he found my mother and me huddled in a closet during a thunderstorm. Entwined with her, I could imagine sitting among the roots of an old oak, talking to the prophetess of old.

My Jewish half grew disproportionately large due to what I saw and heard around me, not as the result of any religious instruction. Hitler liked to shout that Germans were *ein Volk*. Well, Jews were a people, too, I mused, ignorant though I was of any Zionist movement. I accepted as fact my own personal experience; other kids and many adults preferred Wotan and his gang, the Pantheon of the Germanic tribes, because they seemed to enjoy the same games of who could be on top and powerful enough to get rid of their enemies. The other half of me was nurtured by people like Mother Gräfchen and school and even by my mother, who was going to lift us into exalted social circles, as she frequently reminded us.

There were definite advantages in being half and half, though. Whenever one side became too uncomfortable I would retreat to the other and rest easy there for a while. I was aware that, on occasion, joining the Gentile crowd would not always be successful. There were too many Nazis around everywhere. They seemed to have grown like toadstools and mold under tree bark after a humid day. I also knew enough not to expect to be happy on either side. Happiness was for babies who didn't know about death or what people like Mother Gräfchen and her family had been through. Besides, I had heard many sad tales in my hiding place under the long tablecloth, tales far sadder than the stories of the Brothers Grimm or that horrible tale of *Struwelpeter* that Opa Ferdinand read to me at night. I knew life was not meant to be easy. Of course, Mother required me to be happy in her presence and, by and large, I managed to play the part.

I was also aware that somehow our status in life was affected by "Mother's mistake." At first, I thought I might have been the mistake but came to understand that the mistake had been my mother's marriage to my father in America. This new knowledge was quite a relief, though I also entertained a vague notion that one could only be truly loved once one was dead. My other grandmother, Amanda, had a neighbor who was also bringing up her grandchild, so this girl's situation was similar to my own. I had my ears boxed when I mentioned this to my mother, as it turned out that Margot, the girl in question, saw her mother even less than I saw mine and no one knew who her father was. Margot was another child my mother found unsuitable as a playmate and, much to my surprise, so did both my grandmothers. But the two of us still met on the sidewalk from time to time and happily played hopscotch together.

Margot mentioned casually that her mother's "clients" were not so plentiful any more since Hitler established the *Lebensborn*. It was harder for Margot's mother to make a living now. Everyone in my family was horrified when I reported this. Shortly after the shock waves passed, we heard that Margot had died of a brain fever. Suddenly, she was everybody's favorite, and the mother who visited her at most three or four times a year was said to be so devastated by her daughter's death that she had to "go away" for some time.

It seemed a mystery. I could not keep up with grown-ups' thoughts. I had learned from Mother Gräfchen there was a soul which left the body at death and that stayed alive forever in some wonderful place which, to my unsophisticated ear, sounded like a dreadful bore with all those angels and harps and singing and flying around like a flock of starlings. I did not believe that angels could fly very well. In the pictures Mother Gräfchen showed me, the angels were much too heavily laden down with gold harps and gold halos to fly easily. I only had to think of the golden creature I had met at church whose name was Monsignor. He could hardly walk, let alone fly, with all that gold.

Besides, many angels were supposedly not generic ones at all but the souls of dear children, metamorphosed into angels because they had been good. I secretly despised "good," which experience led me to understand as "giving in" to the family or other authorities. Someone always held the upper hand. Still, it shocked me to realize that not all adults were omnipotent, even if they pretended to be. I completely agreed with my grandmother that a woman's lot was particularly hard, what with babies and men demanding that she do unspeakable things and have abortions.

It appeared to me that the outside world was becoming treacherous. Monumental shifts were underway in German society, and the old rules of behavior no longer applied. Respect for one's elders and those with higher social status had eroded and the natural order within families was also being affected. Outside, there were many situations that I could not reconcile with what I was taught.

For instance, my friend Helga and I were all excited about a lesson at school on how to treat animals. Our teacher, Herr Herbst, told us about kennels where abandoned animals could be left and taken care of, doctors who took care of animals instead of people, and of the importance of being kind to all dumb creatures. We were deeply impressed by this lesson because Herr Herbst postulated that animals probably have some kind of soul as well. This made Mother Gräfchen's concept of heaven considerably more interesting. I liked the idea of winged cats and dogs as playmates. I was to become an adult before I realized that the ancient Egyptians already included winged animals in their pantheon of mythical creatures.

In the first grade, it was simply a wonderful idea to play with. But our enjoyment of the lesson had been dampened, literally, by an unfortunate event. One of our classmates, Rachel Morgenstern, not a very pretty girl and not very smart, had wet her pants when Herr Herbst told us about the humane way a sick animal could be put to sleep by poison gas to reawaken in dog heaven. Herr Herbst was incensed that Rachel could not control herself. For a moment, I did not recognize our normally kind and rather placid teacher. His paunch heaved underneath the grey pinstriped tailored suit like a volcano about to erupt. He had a gold pocket watch which we knew to be secure on the little pocket which was its home. It was fastened by a long gold chain that looped across the volcano, and was adorned by a tiny cloisonné locket that boasted a swastika. When Rachel urinated, the locket began a vicious dance on its fetter while Herr Herbst yelled, sweated, groped first for his handkerchief and then his crotch. Rachel's stream was indeed long and full and smelled of mold and earth and cats. As it snaked its way across our gleaming classroom floor, Herr Herbst became even more agitated. He screamed about the need for discipline and that the German people had to be rescued from the impurities of other races. All the while he was kneading his crotch in a distinctly unusual way. His screams brought the head teacher, the Herr Studienrat, from his office. "There, there, Herr Kamerad," he soothed Herr Herbst. "We'll soon see to this."

Rachel, in her agony, tried at first to stem the flow of urine by grabbing her crotch and by jumping up and down while still crouched on her bench. She had black, tightly curled hair which was always full of electricity. Now, it seemed to stand straight on end. She looked like a demented porcupine. Rachel's urine flowed quickly and steamed a little on the cold linoleum floor. Her hand-knitted stockings bagged around her knees and slowly became saturated with urine. She could not stop, nor could she hide her shame. Finally, in utter despair, she grabbed her worn school satchel and tried to run out of the room. Herr Herbst became livid, grabbed her arm and yanked her out of her bench. "Is that what you want, to let everyone know for certain that you are an unclean thing, a Jew?" I decided right there and then to inquire of Herr Herbst why he thought Rachel was unclean. Of course, I would wait until he was less agitated.

Another student, Eva, was dispatched for the janitor, and we continued our lesson while the Herr Studienrat commiserated with Herr Herbst about the rabble they had to teach nowadays. Rachel sat in sullen agony, loudly praying some Hebrew words I recognized: *Baruch atah adonai*. I whispered to Helga that I thought people should come first, before animals, alluding to Rachel, but Helga made believe she didn't understand me.

That afternoon, when we walked home from school, we saw a heavy wagon drawn by two tired-looking horses. The load consisted of many wooden beer barrels, apparently destined for the local pubs, including one that belonged to Helga's family. The horses were strained beyond their endurance. They pulled and tugged until froth appeared on their nostrils, their eyes rolled in ferocious fear, and their tendons seemed ready to burst. The driver used his whip again and again, sometimes viciously using the long leather thongs to hit the creatures' eyes, at other times lashing and cutting their flanks. A rather large wooden branch had fallen from one of the Linden trees which lined the street and had caught under the rear wheels. Helga and I excitedly shouted and pointed to the branch. In answer, he laughed and laid the whip even harder. I couldn't take it any longer. "You torturer of helpless animals," I shouted in my turn. "Don't do that! It is forbidden to torture animals."

The man turned his red blight of a face toward me and, without a word, tightened the horses' reigns and shook his whip at me. We stood transfixed. "Don't do that!" I croaked, frightened this time. He lifted the whip and spat out, "Jew brat!"

Helga pulled me away and we sped home. "How does he know?" I asked Helga. "He delivers beer to our pub," she told me. I felt a wetness pressing down in my underwear. "I won't let it happen," I promised myself. "I am not Rachel."

In the days that followed, I often reminded myself that I was not Rachel. But then who was I? I vaguely knew that such thoughts were unusual for a child to have, but when I said I was an American it was not fun anymore. People either frowned and asked what I was doing in Germany or warned me to go home, wherever that might be.

chapter six
LIFE IS A CIRCUS

Helga and I thought the responses to my country of origin very, very silly. How could something like the name of a country have suddenly become a *"Heil Hitler"* poisoned phrase? We literally fell on the floor laughing and gasping for breath when we came upon a phrase that especially amused us, namely *"Hail Hitler"* instead of *"Hail Mary"* or *"Heil Hitler."* Pauli found us like that one day and shaking his head at so much foolishness, informed us that where he lived with his aunt, children became adults at 14 years of age when they graduated from the eighth grade in public school and were confirmed in the Church. Nowadays this coming-of-age was a time when the family had to decide whether you would have a party at home to celebrate your coming of age, or if you would have a *Jugendfest*, a grander celebration of the transition from being a small fry in the Hitler Youth to becoming a potential member of the Nazi Party. Pauli wasn't sure when you could actually join the real party, but he thought this was absolutely necessary if you wanted to get ahead in the world.

You only had to look at Herr Musterweg as an example of what could happen to you if you did not belong to the NSDAP! Helga wisely nodded. She held the same opinion even though it upset her to think less of her father.

Helga's situation was quite different from Pauli's. She was to be confirmed in the Lutheran church but, of course, could not join the Hitler Youth even though, for most, it had become compulsory. Like me, she had once been refused, when such things were still a matter of choice, and now she hoped that she would be overlooked at the Hitler Youth *Jugendfest* as well. Her hope further cemented our friendship. Helga was always a good girl, did what she was told, and studied hard to get good grades. But she was also intensely loyal and knew her parents would be disappointed in her if she made any move toward separating from them and started to grow up.

Pauli's expectations were strange to me. He still kept talking about having a mother, but none of us, not even he, ever got to see her. He hoped that his sponsors at the local party headquarters would help him to participate in the mass coming-of-age party for Hitler Youth. He thought it would be such fun to jump over a bonfire, to sing songs in the middle of the night, and to be allowed to drink beer right in front of everybody because you were now grown up. Pauli had managed to join a troop but was not a valued member. He was quiet about what he did at the headquarters. Helga and I knew that whatever he did was forbidden and he cringed if we asked, so we stopped talking about it, though we were burning to know the details. Besides, he was the only other child who wanted to play with us.

As for myself, I knew my life would be very different. My grandparents and my mother expected me to go on to the Lyceum (the high school for girls) after completion of the fourth grade. An examination would have to be passed and there would be a monthly tuition fee. I knew that there was a sudden exchange of letters between my parents. Mother was furious, as usual. It seemed my father in America thought that because I was a girl I didn't have to go to high school. As an alternative, I could take an apprenticeship somewhere as he had done. "And look where it got him," my mother grimly remarked. "He can't make a living, even in America." Much to my surprise Oma Anna agreed with her this time. They also agreed that my friends Pauli and Helga were already much too "set in their ways," meaning they knew more or less where their lives were expected to lead them. I on the other hand, hadn't the faintest notion of where I would be at the end of the fourth grade, though I didn't doubt I would pass the examination.

Herr Herbst, still our classroom teacher, expressed confidence that I would do well and bring honor to him and his class. He seemed to have forgotten that I was Jewish and was proud of me. Only about one third of our class of 25 girls was expected to pass. Helga would go to middle school (*Mittelschule*), where she would learn something useful, her father explained to us, something that would allow her to make a living. He wanted her to be a nurse or a kindergarten teacher, maybe even a secretary, but for that he would have to pay extra, as secretaries were expected to know a foreign language. "Of course with the way things are going, everyone will have to learn German," he said, not entirely in jest. He had begun to find some like-minded men among his steady customers. "You are spoiling that kid of yours. Let her get married and have kids. I hear the *Kinderbeiscuss* [a sum paid each family birth until a child reached 14] is large enough so that a guy can stop working after the fifth one. Does your old woman still bleed? Go to it, man."

Helga and I were mortified. Some of the older kids had told us about the "monthlies" and how they had to be tamed with crochet containers stuffed with rags and cotton. Helga and I both had seen pails of bloody water in the toilets of our apartments. But we didn't make the connection to either babies or to our mothers. Helga was really upset. "Your mother probably bleeds and tries to make babies. My mother and father wouldn't think of such a thing." I could not imagine Herr and Frau Musterweg as makers of babies either, but secretly admired my mother's glamorous ways even though nobody I knew shared my admiration.

Helga tried to force me into a pact which stipulated that neither one of us should have babies. I was reluctant to go along with her suggestion. However, I liked her notion that it would be easier for me to stay childless due to the fact that I was slated for the Lyceum, where I would learn useless things like foreign languages and read classic books. All the men in the pub disliked "intellectual assholes." I knew enough about human anatomy to find "assholes" an incorrect description but did not want to argue with Helga because her parents had not asked what she wanted to do. She was given no choice. While nobody had asked me either, I knew that eventually I would be consulted. At that particular moment my mother was content to fret about the fact that I needed glasses. My grandparents thought I looked like a "cute scholar," whereas Mother worried I would turn out to be a "bluestocking." It all sounded grim to me.

Things had changed. The police were no longer reliable protectors. Some of them made a specialty of befriending children, but Helga and I soon realized they were spying on us. They wanted us to tell them what Helga's father and Opa Ferdinand talked about. We reported our discovery to Anna and to Helga's parents. Their responses differed greatly. Anna said the police had been infiltrated by the Nazis. She warned us that, perhaps, some of the new policemen liked children too much. We were never to accept any gifts from them and never to stay alone with any of them. Helga and I worried what we should do if we were ever to be approached. After all, they were police and had the power. We heard from other children that they had been taken to a cellar where they were given hot chocolate and candy. Then they had to pull their pants down.

Pauli knew firsthand about the cellar. He had received a pocket knife for pulling down his pants. In fact, he had been in the cellar several times, each time with a different policeman. They had asked many questions, he said, a real interrogation, and some of them liked to touch his front. He didn't mind because they also let him use the bathroom, which had a faucet for hot water. He could use the hot water as much as he liked even if he had nothing to tell them or didn't want to pull his pants down. When Helga and I asked why the hot water meant so much to him, he explained how nice it was to have hot water from a faucet instead of waiting until it heated up in a pot, as they did at his home.

Despite these upheavals, Oma Anna continued her efforts to make my childhood tranquil and happy, though it was difficult for her to accept the sudden transformation that had taken place among her neighbors and friends. And in truth, Oma had changed a lot. She had become irritable and tried to stay on the move all day long. My appetite for the visually exciting had been stimulated by Mother Gräfchen's collection of prayer cards and by the repeated visits to her church. But Oma wasn't comfortable there. Instead, she collected Helga, Pauli, and me and took us on the tram to the museums on the Island of Museums in the middle of Berlin. There we beheld an entire Greek temple, the Pergamon Altar. During one of our visits, we met an old gentleman who explained that this beautiful building had been stolen by the Germans from the Greeks and reassembled here. He said this extra loud so that the guards would hear it. Oma Anna cautioned, "They'll put you in jail for saying that." To which he raised his fists and shouted, "The truth will out!" I felt as though he were looking for a person named Truth, as he stood there like Moses immediately after he received the Ten Commandments. Next to the Pergamon was the wall and city entrance of Babylon, the Babylon from the same Bible both grandmothers knew so well.

This gentleman became our constant companion. He waited

for us on Wednesday afternoons when entrance to the museums was free. We brought a sandwich and cake for him. The bunch of us would sit on the shore of the canal surrounding the Isle of Museums, a tributary of the river Spree, and drink sweetened coffee with a lot of milk in it. Municipal benches, some given to the people of the city by prominent Jewish families, made such al fresco feasts pleasant. Our friend's named, so he told us, was an old and distinguished one: Mathias auf der Heyde. He billed himself a dispossessed *Freiherr* (a fairly low rank among the aristocracy), a scholar of ancient history, and an enemy of Hitler. All this endeared him to Oma Anna, who had a soft spot in her heart for all sad and displaced or hurt creatures.

Mathias auf der Heyde was a splendid scarecrow indeed. He sported flowing cravats and wore loose smocks or old-fashioned tailored suits with a pinched-in waist. He did not seem out of place on our picnics, adding his pleasure to ours. He explained in detail how the Pergamon had been stolen by amateur German anthropologists, and didn't really belong to the great German people. He explained how the temple had once stood on a hill overlooking the bright blue sea. I envisioned how graceful and happy the people there must have been to have built such a temple.

I only knew the grim North Sea off the northeast tip of Germany, where my mother and I had once had a brief holiday. A storm was brewing and the waves were fairly high but mother kept an eye on me from a boardwalk. When I looked up at her for approval, I saw what she called a "businessman" leaning toward her. I raced out of the water and, when mother introduced me, butted my head into his stomach. He gasped and fell down. I inadvertently sprinkled sand and water on his "good suit" as he moaned, rising bedraggled from the wooden floor. Mother was furious. "You lost me a good commission," she said. But I felt that man had no business interfering with my brief holiday with mother. Now, looking at the Pergamon and placing my mind's eye on the bright blue sea around it, I felt certain that nobody who had to contend with the North Sea could have built such a beautiful place.

Pauli didn't want to do such sissy things as go to museums until Mathias showed him all the huge canvases in the Deutsche Museum, hall after hall of giant depictions of war. I always had to sneeze there, the air was so dry. And even Oma Anna, who was a real enthusiast when it came to art, couldn't stand it for too long. Eventually, Pauli went through those halls by himself while Mathias bought his "women friends" ice cream that dripped down our fronts until we no longer qualified as good museums visitors.

When Helga and I went to clean ourselves up one of the toilet attendants took a shine to us. She was buxom and red-faced with a puny grey chignon spilling greasy strands of hair onto her shoulders. "You young ladies havin' fun? Spoilt, I say, is what you are. Me, I never seen a place like this from the inside until I started to work here. And then I only have time to wipe other people's piss!" She laughed uproariously, then suddenly fell silent. Worshipfully, she shouted, "And *Der Führer* made it possible for me to sit while I work. He took pity on the old so we can die in peace. That man is our savior." Fortunately, Anna came in and rescued us, but we didn't get away until the *Toilettendame* had made us give the Hitler Salute.

Mathias did not like Pauli. "He has been corrupted beyond repair," he informed Anna. "He should not be around the girls." Anna disagreed. "He is just an abandoned child; he will be all right with a little care." But she was not as feisty as she sounded. Her preoccupation with my friends and me had taken on a driven, agitated quality. She rounded us up constantly to keep us out of trouble and forbade us to speak with strangers.

We also visited the famous Berlin Zoo. Anna told me that my mother used to enjoy taking me there before she became "high and mighty." Apparently, I had facilitated her meeting her future husband, Waldemar Friedrich von Udebek, during one of our visits. I had stuck out even then, with my pitch black hair and smocks so short one could see my matching underwear. My finery was handmade for me by my mother and by Oma Amanda, who would have another fit had she known I helped my mother to meet men other than my father. The man we met was not yet "Uncle Walt," but he was amused when I declared loudly that I liked the crocodiles best of all the animals. My mortified mother tried to stop me but, slobbering ice cream all over myself, I continued to describe the superior qualities of the crocs.

It turned out that Walt too had come to the zoo to eat the famous ice cream, and he made friends with me. Since I usually disliked strangers, especially male strangers who seemed attracted to my mother, all three of us were in fine spirits. Later, when mother and I joined the Udebeck clan, another more suitable and dignified story of their meeting was concocted. But in the meantime, Oma Anna, Helga, Pauli, and I loved to hear the original version.

We also went to the Planetarium in the *Tiergarten*, Berlin's largest park. We saw Leni Riefenthal's film of the 1936 Olympics with Hitler ranting and raving right into her face while she directed her camera crew. Later, she claimed innocence of Hitler's aims. We also saw *Ratsel der Urwald Holle* (The Riddle of the Hellish Jungle). We liked that one better because the women had naked breasts and long hair. The only one who did not care for the group outings was Opa Ferdinand. We children minded our manners and did not make nasty remarks about "Mathias the Noble," as Ferdinand wryly called him. Ferdinand did not like being friendly with someone who had a title. But Mathias held the same political views as he did, something that was hard to understand among the men of our neighborhood, especially the die-hard Social Democrats. "Damned aesthete," Ferdinand snorted when we reported on our outings. But that only made Helga and me like and trust Mathias all the more.

Mathias was present when a little circus came to our neighborhood. Oma and Mother Gräfchen were delighted. In their youth at the Polish-German border there had been many such traveling performers. Many were gypsies. They set up for their show on Herr Grau's large property, using his loading platform as a stage of sorts. Several rows of clumsy folding chairs and benches were set up by the strong man of the group while a gaunt young woman strung a wire between portable poles. One pole was higher than the other, though the wire was strung evenly at the same height.

Both Oma Anna and Mother Gräfchen could hardly wait for evening when the show was to begin. It was a Saturday night, and all the men were home from work. Most of the women had already picked up their baking sheets from the shop of baker Kern, where they earlier brought their yeast or fruit cakes to bake in the even heat of his large brick oven. Much to Oma's amusement, the Jewish families on our block also brought their *Shabbos Cholent* (a traditional Shabbos stew) to bake there and then had young Christian boys, their *Shabbos Goyim*, pick them up in time for their meal. Oma Anna snorted: "It's not kosher to cook in a Goy's oven and then to make believe they are holier than we are because I cook for my family on Saturdays. Hypocrites." Opa Ferdinand grinned when she carried on like that. He pinched her behind until she giggled like a young girl and slapped his hand. "Not in front of the child," she grinned back.

On the night the circus came to Grau's place all such thoughts were forgotten. The super pious among Anna's fellow Jews would not come to the performance anyway, not only because it was Shabbat but also because they were forbidden to see the body of a woman clad only in leotard. Nevertheless, when Anna, Helga, Pauli, and I came down at dusk to attend the performance we saw some of the Jewish children, all boys, hiding behind the stacks of coal and wood. We had tried several times to make friends with them, but they had run away. At least none of them called me "foreigner" or shoved me like the German children in the playground.

We sat expectantly, eating some of Anna's apple cake. We noticed that the audience consisted primarily of women and children. Expectation of something wondrous about to happen cloaked the evening. A handsome, decidedly un-Aryan young man in a gaudy get up of tight red satin pants and black silk shirt began to play the violin. Looking around myself I surmised that all shared my happy thoughts. This was even better than listening to the opera with Opa Ferdinand!

As I settled into the soft murmur of the crowd, waiting for the performance to start, I saw that Pauli was missing. Scanning the crowd, I saw him furtively opening the door of one of the wooden caravans and sliding inside. I got up to wave him back. The performance was about to begin! The young woman we had seen before with the high wire was back, this time in a glittering suit with her long black hair streaming down her back. I was frantic about Pauli, but Oma Anna pulled me down and hushed me. "It's alright," she whispered.

I didn't know what to do. Should I run after Pauli, who had definitely crept into one of the gypsy wagons? What was he doing there? I felt it was a bit of gall for him to enter such foreign households. I was jealous, too, as I found roaming gypsies very appealing. I was especially fascinated by the rumor that, on occasion, they would grab and abduct a child, who would never be heard from again. When Oma Amanda threatened sometimes that she would sell me to the gypsies if I didn't behave, I held my breath, hoping that she would make good on her threat. I had seen gypsies' caravans parked on the festival grounds of Oma Amanda's vegetable garden association. Could it be that Pauli had made a deal with the gypsies to carry him off?

For a moment I feared that the whole ugly scene around

me was just a diversion to enable Pauli to mount one of his scenes, like when he threatened Helga and me with un-Aryan spinsterhood. But in looking for Pauli I noticed something else. Herr Grotke and a group of Brownshirts were questioning Herr Grau and the director of the circus. That worthy gent, already in his ringmaster's costume, kept pointing to a crumpled piece of paper. I couldn't hear what he was saying, but I couldn't help turning away from the performance to see what Grotke and his men were doing.

The woman with the long hair had wrapped it tightly around a hook that was suspended from the wire. She whirred down toward the lower of the two poles she had set up before. The music reached a crashing crescendo and the audience clapped excitedly – this at the very time two brawny Brownshirts were exerting themselves to disengage the pole toward which the woman on the hook was hurtling. Herr Grau, the Circus Master, and a few men in the audience ran and climbed over and through the staggered row of seats in order to stop the mayhem that was about to ensue. The women shrieked, someone tripped Herr Grau so that he fell into the laps of some of his customers, and children began to cry. The Circus Master suddenly stopped running; he seemed near a heart attack, breathing heavily, and shouting: "You swine! I have a legal document that permits my artists to perform here."

Grotke became huffy. "I'm sure you did not receive a permission to perform on ground belonging to a Jew. We should take you into custody and put you in jail."

"You just do that," the Master shouted back. "I'll show your precious Office of Working Permits how often I gave you a tip."

And then Grotke: "And then we'll have you on bribery charges, you son of a whore. You and all of your gypsies will sit in jail till Kingdom come. I will personally see to it."

I could not follow their shouting match any longer. The shrieks and cries of the crowd directed my attention back to the ring and the two poles. The two Brownshirts were holding down the hysterical performer, who tried to squirm away from them. She bit them, and they landed some openhanded blows on her. Most of the women had grabbed their children and tried either to shield them from the scene before them or to leave altogether. But the Brownshirts did not let anyone pass. Their commander shouted something about "crowd control." A few of them formed a wedge-shaped group and silently, menacingly, marched toward the frightened, pleading, desperate crowd. The two Brownshirts who were beating up the acrobat were by now really enjoying themselves. They shouted to their comrades to come and join in the fun. "Look at the doll jiggling," one of them laughed. The column of men who had listened to their commander halted so abruptly that those in back stumbled. Some fell on top of those in front of them.

A small gap between the larger group of Brownshirts and those intent on brawling opened up. A few of the women managed to flee. The small number of men in the audience had disappeared as if by magic. I saw Frau Breitenbach shake a fist at the back of her husband. Anna, aghast at the assault, cried: "Help her. Why doesn't someone help her?" Mathias, who had joined us wearing a very fancy vest under his shabby waist coat and a pleated shirt, pushed her down and clamped his hand over her mouth. "Shh," he hissed. "This time they'll make *Hackepeter* (minced meat) out of you for sure. They know you are a troublemaker." Anna was indignant. "You are a fine one to talk. You are always provoking them." "Dear lady," he replied, "that is all I can do, but you . . . you have the child and the women in your practice who rely on you." He placed himself in such a way that Anna's view was blocked. But I saw how the Brownshirts were ripping the glittering leotard off the struggling girl's body. The entire cohort was in turmoil, with some of the men still striving to reach their colleagues, others trying to prevent them from doing so, and their commander shouting for them all to return to formation.

The situation was out of control. Perhaps now was the time

to rescue Pauli from the wagon into which he had vanished. The tumultuous noise around me rose to ever louder proportions. Some of the women were not as meek as the Brownshirts had expected them to be. Half a dozen of them were trying to pull the two bullies away from the slender acrobat. Two women with balled fists beat them soundly on their chests. One woman who had stood on the sidelines until then somehow reached the center of the brawling and unbuckled the tight black leather belts holding up the would-be molesters' uniform pants so that they fell around their knees. Not only did their naked behinds show, but everyone started to laugh at them. By the time they noticed what had happened the women had pushed them to the ground and were sitting on them. Grotke and the Circus Master were still arguing although by now the police had arrived and tried to soothe everyone's tempers. But neither the Circus Master nor Grotke had any intention of giving in. While Grotke yelled about his principles, which were the same as *Der Führer's*, the Circus Master yelled about his status as a legitimate performing foreigner who had the right to be treated courteously.

Everyone was so fascinated by this spectacle that no one in the crowd noticed that one of the caravans was slowly rolling toward the open exit door at the other end of the lot. I jumped up and tried to wrestle myself out of Oma Anna's arms. I was certain it was the very caravan that Pauli had climbed into. Helga and I at last freed ourselves and ran as fast as we could to catch up with the vehicle. But by now the horses had been given their leads and begun to run. It became impossible to catch up, but not impossible to see who was looking out of the small window that was cut into the door. It was Pauli, all right. Helga and I were both out of breath and started to cry. When Anna and Mathias found us, they didn't ask us why we were crying but took us home without delay and made some cocoa for us. Opa Ferdinand was fast asleep.

The next morning, Anna let me know she understood what

had gone on. "Don't worry about Pauli," she said as she stroked my hair. "His mother came for him after all." But Helga and I did worry and regretted missing the chance to meet Pauli's mother. The next time I heard about Pauli was after the war ended. He, his mother, and their clan had all been gassed in one of the extermination camps in Eastern Europe.

chapter seven
BROADENING HORIZONS

Helga and I made a sorry twosome after losing our friend in what we thought of as a romantic manner. Helga had less time for me because she had to go to religious school, but she did accompany Oma and me, and sometimes Mathias auf der Heyde, to cultural films. We had gone to movies before, and *Ratsel der Urwaldhölle* (Mysteries of the Jungle Hell) was a favorite for Helga and me because the women had very long hair and went about naked. It was a welcome opportunity for us to study the female anatomy, a subject that had become taboo since we were about eight years old. We often speculated why it was all right to talk about it before then, when even "penis" and "vagina" were not dirty words. Pauli had been an invaluable and interested informant during such debates. If only we knew where he was! Oma Anna and Mathias preferred such epics as Riefenstahl's *Olympics*. The opus bored me to tears because I could see no good reason for dozens of people running around in circles or forming letters with their bodies or waving flags around. I liked the gymnasts and sprinters, though.

Perhaps due to the atmosphere created by the Olympics, my mother had a new enthusiasm: "Modern Health," which included eating lots of salad and sunbathing in the nude. Opa Ferdinand called it "rabbit food" and disdained any form of Modern Health, especially because it required giving up his *Stammtisch* beer and his wine with dinner. As part of her new interest, Mother wanted me to join a gymnastic class after I told her I liked to dance.

By this time, Herr Schloscke had driven me to the Opera House many times. It seemed that my third grandmother-to-be ("Uncle" Walt Udebeck's mother) didn't care for dance, but she had a permanent "loge." Later, I heard her complain that the loge "cost a fortune, but what could one do? One needed the loge." I still don't really know what she "needed" the expensive seats for other than listening to music. She loved opera and symphonies but dance gave her a headache. Since nobody else in the family liked dance either, I was dispatched with Schloscke, who waited for me outside. A large pink bow fastened to the top of my pitch black hair, wearing a wine red velvet dress, I felt like a princess. Some of the neighborhood kids came to see me off and giggled at my attire and my attendant.

Little did my soon-to-be step-grandmother know what she had wrought with her well-meant present. I became an impassioned admirer of dance, classic ballet in particular, because it soothed me to behold such perfection. However, I shuddered when I saw Wigman's *Hexentanz* (Witch's Dance) and Kreutzberg's *Totentanz* (Dance of Death). I entertained enough scary feelings during my everyday life with Anna; I didn't want to feel them during my splendid solo outings.

Of course I was not entirely alone. There was Schloske, after all. He was a kind man who bought expensive bars of chocolate for me when he saw me upset by a performance, patted my head just behind the big pink bow and muttered: *"det arme Kind muss sich ja wohl janz alehne fuhlen da drinne"* (the poor child must feel so lonely in there). He spoke in Berlin dialect, a language I was forbidden to speak because, according to my mother, it would immediately reveal that I was not well brought up and cast shame on her. When I pointed out that my beloved behavior and speech couldn't possibly be her fault since it was Oma Anna and Opa Ferdinand who had taught me, she hauled me off and slapped me across the mouth. "Ungrateful wretch," she hissed.

Oma Anna was very ambivalent about my cultural outings. Although she supported my wish to dance, she thought it might be overstimulating for me to be exposed to adult drama. I was amazed when she said so, as we had plenty of drama in our house. Anna explained that what we experienced at home was *Realität* against which one could defend oneself. In contrast, she said, the emotions evoked during theatrical performances left the audience at the mercy of the artists. She pointed out that I often came home overwrought and excited because a ballerina had died so beautifully or had stood on her toes until thunderous applause pushed her off again. I desperately wanted to walk on my toes as well. I did not agree with Oma Anna, who was kindness personified and helped anyone who needed it. She never hit me. But since the experience with my mother – when she slapped my face after I told her about her "mistake" – I had become cautious. I decided not to tell her that Frau Grotke's short-lived pregnancy, Pauli's escape and, above all, Fraulein Inglemeier's suicide had been much more painful to me than I had let on. Just thinking about these scenes made me want to cry and caused my skin to pucker into tiny goose bumps.

So now, when I told my mother about the wonders of dancing, she enrolled me in a gym class that served her new ideal of Modern Health. The whole neighborhood chuckled and made remarks when I appeared in a Gymnastic *Anzug* (gym suit), swinging my *Kulturbeutel* (literally my "bag of culture," my gym bag) that contained my special shoes, soap, and towel.

Oma Amanda thought it was downright decadent to have all the little girls bathe so often. After all, they might "touch themselves" after showering together.

My gym lessons evoked another storm among the women who had daughters. Some felt it would be cheaper to let their girls go to the *Jungmädel*, to join the young Nazi girls. They would get the same gym instruction there without the unhealthy showers that would make everyone catch cold. Also, their daughters would learn some of the "modern" ways of living, which in this setting meant being a Nazi, without all the fuss. My major disappointment was that the gym suit, which had been purchased at considerable expense on the *Kurfursten Damm* (the equivalent of New York's Fifth Avenue), was cut exactly like those worn by Olympic athletes. I thought it was ugly. What I wanted was a tutu and pointed shoes. But I had to pursue Modern Health instead.

I also missed Helga. She often sat at the table by the large windows of the pub doing her homework and committing large portions of the New Testament to memory. She furtively waved to me and mouthed soundless words to me. When it became cold, we fared better. She learned *Spiegelschrift* (mirror writing) and wrote messages to me with the condensation that coated the window. I was lonely. Despite being the center of the local women's group, Anna had changed. She talked a great deal about what Opa Ferdinand called *"Unsinn"* (nonsense). Sometimes she forgot to cook dinner and then rushed around, trying to make up time, even though Opa and I were prepared to wait. We both knew something was wrong and thought it had something to do with "the times," meaning the frustrating surveillance under which we all lived. I was continuously full of unease and tried not to imagine how I would act if someone came to take Oma away.

Helga and I still met in school, so I was able to enlist her in a plan to keep Oma safe. I did not even trust Mathias. At any rate, I suggested to the sad and now lethargic Anna that she come to school with Helga and me and sit on the benches in the local public square, *Gustaf Adolf Platz*, where she used to take me to play in the sandbox. It was ideally situated right across the embankment of the *Landwehrkanal* where our school was located. She would wait from 8 a.m. until noon, read a paper, or do some knitting. She made friends with the pigeons and assorted babies and their mothers. Her only complaint was that the young mothers were "too rough with the babies," letting them cry too long and not letting her pick them up and soothe them. As long as the weather held, this plan worked just fine. Mathias von der Heyde helped by coming by every once in a while to keep Anna company, sometimes to whisper more secrets to her. She always seemed agitated after his visits.

I thought of confiding some of Oma Anna's strange behavior to my mother but decided against it. Mathias seemed a more likely confidant, but he was too preoccupied with delivering all sorts of odd and ends to my grandparents to pay as much attention to me as he previously had. I wondered if he had become some kind of delivery man. He always seemed to be carrying large bundles and told Oma things about the gypsies' market that I was not supposed to hear. I made as blank a face as I could and made believe that I hadn't heard how Arnie Kleingold had been beaten or how Rifke Kunsberg had disappeared, leaving her two infant children behind. Her husband Nat had already been taken by the secret police, the Gestapo, and she was still nursing her babies at the time of her disappearance, so there was little reason not to assume the worst. Mathias spent that week running around to see if he could find a wet nurse for the infants and, to everyone's amazement, he found one from nearby Spreewald, a town known to have the healthiest women for hire.

Mathias found an empty apartment in a good neighborhood. The previous inhabitants had been "resettled" and the word was not yet out among those Nazis looking for more elegant quarters. The woman Mathias had found agreed to stay in the apartment by herself, provided that someone brought her food three times a day and did the babies' diapers. Her own 12-year-old son came with her and was to keep an eye on her own toddler. This highly unusual arrangement was agreed upon with large sums of money appearing from nowhere, and from no one I had ever heard of before. Some outfit called "Jews for Zion" was the sponsor, and the woman in question, it turned out, agreed to the assignment because she felt akin to the Jews she was now serving.

Before the dark days when Mathias, as so many others, disappeared out of my life, Anna and I learned to lean on him with our worries. He was quite certain that my mother was none of the things the neighbors claimed she was. "She is a woman of the world and concerned for you," he kept reiterating. That simple sentence reassured us. Still, he had never met Mother, so how could he be sure about this?

"Why couldn't she have hooked up with someone like Mathias?" Oma Anna sighed. "He is of the upper world she wants to climb into." Opa Ferdinand laughed until he was beet red and had to drink an extra beer when we talked to him about Mathias. "Two strikes against your precious friend. He is only half a man and he has no money," he finally sputtered. Oma Anna seemed to have an insight about Mathias right there and then. "Maybe *that's* why his family doesn't want him," she suggested. I gathered that *"that's"* referred to homosexuality. Even though I didn't know the word then, I had learned from Pauli that some men only liked other men and therefore wanted to marry them.

This did not seem unreasonable to me as, from all that I heard under the tablecloth, men and women had a hard time with each other. Maybe, if a couple was like each other, they would fight less. Pauli had managed to discuss the subject in this manner, swearing me to secrecy. "The Nazis don't allow it. You better tell that guy who hangs out with us to be careful."

"Why?" I wanted to know. "He doesn't want to marry any of us," I tried to reassure Pauli. And the fact was that Oma Anna and I needed someone with whom we could talk about our feelings. In contrast to Opa Ferdinand, who came home slightly inebriated almost daily now, Mathias was always ready to sip coffee with us and talk, although we no longer went to the museums and movies. We either stayed home or found a place on the *Landwehrkanal* where we could dangle our feet in the water and find some peace.

There was always tension in the air at that time and the reports of people vanishing increased. Oma Anna and I realized that things for Opa Ferdinand were very difficult. He didn't want to leave us and return to Switzerland, but the pressures on him to become a German citizen were becoming greater at his place of work. He didn't like having to produce what looked to him like pieces of weapons. And by now his group of Social Democrats had disbanded, the members having only brief and secret contact with one another. But even with grumpy, demanding Ferdinand, Mathias showed understanding. "He has many problems, poor man. He could escape from this rats' nest but doesn't want to leave you. And if he did, they would find out that your mother was really born in Poland and is far from Aryan," he added. I chose to ignore him. Things were going pretty nicely for me, I thought.

At my Modern Health Club I had met a few girls who also felt their parents were "drips." One of them was a fine acrobat, who showed me some of the things she could do and, lo and behold, I turned out to be *gelenkig* (flexible). But when I showed my mother my new tricks, she declared them "not nice." I looked like a pretzel, she remarked. Besides, I had always been clumsy. How could I suddenly be so flexible? Mathias, on the other hand, was pleased. He gave me some advice during one of the few times when he spoke of his own past life. "Try to make friends with a girl who takes dancing lessons to show you the basic exercises. They like their girls to be graceful where your mother wants to go," he remarked.

All the girls in Modern Health took some kind of dancing lessons, but only one, a girl thin as a reed and with very red hair, took ballet. She was overjoyed to teach me everything she learned and pointed out to me the good teachers who had come straight from the revered Russian School or from the Berlin Opera House where, surprisingly, they were now leaning toward modern dance. I knew what she was talking about. What joy! I felt I finally belonged to a group of like-minded people, even if it was only a group of two. I gratefully submitted to my strict ballet mistress, one Gabriella von Rudighorn, who was no doubt imitating a once great ballerina, or so her imperious mien suggested. Mathias applauded and mother sneered. Occasionally Oma Amanda too expressed approval, though she worried that dancing might bring me in touch with "ungodly" people from theater.

Uncle Walt had become more and more of a presence in my life. I became grateful to him instead of rebuking him and provoking my mother. I realized one boring afternoon that all my "good toys" were gifts from him. He had bought me a cuddly baby doll with a big head and a soft body on a trip to a *Weihnachtsmarkt* (Christmas market) some years before, and, at the same market, I saw a wind-up doll that cried and waved its limbs when wound up; he bought it for me as well. For my birthday, there was a doll carriage and a cradle. My mother protested, but what could she do? Walt was nice to me, so I accepted him as a "good guy." He also gave me a wristwatch when I was six years old, an unheard of luxury for a small child in those days. And, of course there were the many times I was allowed to come to his family's compound on the Havel, one of the idyllic waterways that surround Berlin. The Udebeck's property in Kapberg was right where the river widened into a lake and encompassed an old plum orchard which ended up in a narrow strip of lawn that led directly to the water. Cement steps opened up to the dock where a motor boat, a canoe, a sailboat, and an old fishing tub were moored. A very old farmer's house was beautifully renovated in such a manner that the ancient façade of the house continued to face the street but hid how comfortable it was and how lavishly it had been restored.

Mother was usually in a good mood when she went to Kapberg and turned only slightly sour when I was to go along. I didn't particularly want to go. Visiting Oma Amanda and Opa Christian on the weekend appealed to me much more than having to curtsy to all sorts of people I neither knew nor, on closer acquaintance, liked very much. I was the only child around. What I wanted was someone to talk to who would help me understand the behavior of the visitors. The weekend crowd usually arrived in the late afternoon. They were young men and women "on their way up." Most of the girls flirted with Maximilian, Walt's older brother. He was reported on occasion to have become so enamored of a young lady that he found her a flat or a job at the same time as he vouched for her virginity to her parents. It was a great joke to all when they speculated how he could know such intimate details. He also helped along the young men who visited, though I was not sure in what ways. Recalling my talks with Pauli and Helga of how success in life meant belonging to the party, I was not surprised that most of the guests were staunch Nazis and even showed up for the weekend in their SA or SS uniforms. The only non-Nazi was Walt.

I had never been in such close proximity to the feared and despised Nazis. Here at Kapberg they were just a bunch of young folks letting go of the tensions of their work week which, back then, was five-and-a-half or six days. Maximilian was revered by the Nazis. He had been among their early supporters and was seen by them as an intellectual visionary. Having been present when Maximilian and Walt yelled at each other over political issues, I knew that the older brother was despised by his extended family for precisely these views. Walt was decidedly against the Nazis and all they stood for, and Maximilian was beside himself over Walt's opposition. "Opa Ferdinand would want to kill this guy," I thought. Nor was Maximilian well-disposed toward me. He called me the "elephant with wings," and as the cartoon character Dumbo had not yet been created, the crowd was thrilled with the originality of my nickname. I felt more of an outsider than ever.

The Saturday crowd was usually dirty and sweaty upon arrival. Nevertheless, there was a lot of hugging and backslapping, everybody exclaiming about the pleasant surprise of meeting each other on the train while Maximilian's wife, Kundchen, ran around fetching towels and cold drinks. I felt they all couldn't be very bright, since they took the same train each week. So why was it so "deliciously surprising" to repeat the same meeting each week? No wonder they needed Maximilian's help! To make themselves comfortable they either took a swim or an outdoor shower on the dock off of which people swam. To me showering was altogether new. It seemed horrendously wasteful, but then I figured that Maximilian and Kundchen could no doubt afford the water bill and didn't have to catch rain water in a barrel like Oma and Opa Letz.

The fact that people showered every day, sometimes even twice a day, puzzled me. I took to hanging around when these acquaintances showered outside under the large spigot, which sometimes stopped spraying. They all tended to do this in the nude or in very skimpy bathing suits. Skimpy meant that the ladies wore no bras and the gentlemen made do with a towel around their often copious midriffs. I watched with interest when a group of three of four arrived; I wanted to monitor what it was that needed such urgent ablutions. I discovered that many of the things Pauli had told me were true. People did have hair in unmentionable places and under their arms. My mother received complaints. The free-love-modern-health advocates were embarrassed by my interest in their bodies. I was told not to show my face again when adults were using the outdoor shower. I was insulted and said so. My mother, her face inflated into a purple balloon, dragged me into the house and into our room and forbade me to come out until she gave me permission. So I was under house arrest until the following day, Sunday, when the crowd took off and returned to Berlin.

Thankfully, Mathias made himself available. He must have sensed that I would get myself into trouble. He agreed that it was interesting to find out what people looked like, but also felt it would have been smarter not to be so open about it and, above all, not to shame my mother. "It's hard enough for her to keep you with her in that set-up," he explained. "You mustn't make it harder for her." When he mentioned that the crowd probably belonged to both the Nazi party and the Modern Health Movement, I was horrified. "Don't be, little one," he stroked my hair. "That's the way to survive." Survive? I didn't know why this group of fancy people, as my grandparents no doubt termed them, should be in danger of being killed, but from Mathias's face and tone of voice I knew he spoke the truth. But I had learned by that time that truth was not the same for everybody.

Mathias and Helga were of the same opinion: Walt wanted to marry my mother and I was part of the deal. My heart pounded. I felt sick. Despite Walt's friendliness, I didn't want anybody besides my father in America to be my father. Oma Amanda would not like it, I feared, and she was more important to me. Besides, Maximilian and Walt were forever fighting about the Nazis because Walt simply wouldn't join the party, despite the fact that his older brother practically ordered him to do so. Indeed, Maximilian thought it particularly important that Walt be a party member if he married my mother. The two of them set to with their opposing arguments, sitting near the water where they thought nobody could hear them. In fact, the whole neighborhood watched when the two marched agitatedly into the back and started to shout. When

I managed to slip away, I went and looked at the spectacle of grown men rolling down a hill and then getting up, lurching and huffing and puffing like steam engines. I didn't find it very funny or very interesting. Having retrieved Opa Ferdinand from his pub, I had seen many people act the same way, and they didn't have to contend with gaping strangers or sand on their clothes. When someone in the neighborhood was that drunk, people on our street discreetly turned away. They had no wish to shame one other.

But there was something I hadn't told even Mathias. I saw my neighbors selling things on the promenade of my local neighborhood, clowns on sticks, candied apples and all the glorious glittery junk of a carnival. And I had heard only too often how much money it cost to educate me and keep me fed and clothed. So I decided that I too would sell something on the promenade.

But what? Nobody seemed interested in the gladiolas that bloomed so brightly and full of flash in the Udebeck compound. The very next time I was among the invited guests, I deftly cut a couple dozen of the stately flowers and proceeded to carry them up the hill. Before I got there Walt caught me. "What in the world are you doing?" he gasped. "Bruno the gardener saw you. Are you going to a funeral?" "No," I answered truthfully. "I wanted to sell them and make some money. We need it."

Walt tried hard not to let me see that he thought I was funny. Not so my mother. I got a good hiding while she shrieked, "I will beat the last Jewish trait out of you." I had to ask Matthias what she meant. My feelings hurt no less than my bottom.

Gradually my mother's status at the gatherings changed. Now it was she who made the menus, dealt with the tradesmen, and offered cool drinks to arriving visitors. Kundchen, Maximilian's wife, hung around like a beagle that had lost its master. The young ladies who had previously ignored me suddenly determined that I would look just adorable in a dirndl dress. The next week they showed up with one and dressed me up in it. For some reason unknown to me, this was to be a present for Maximilian. But when they paraded me in front of him, he became enraged. "It was bad manners, not to say unkind, to strew salt into a person's wounds. Take the child away," he thundered. Apparently, it was bad taste to dress an American-Jewish child in *treudeutsche* (truly German) clothing. Mathias thought I must be wrong when I told him that Maximilian's temper tantrum, in my opinion, had to do with his relationship to my beautiful mother. He also, for the first time, made a remark to me that was not warm and supportive. "I imagine your precocity finally got to them. Between you and Maximilian they felt stripped." I took off my dirndl and threw it at him and, with as much dignity as I could muster, stalked out of the room.

Mother and I had been able to take an earlier train to Kapberg because school closed after two hours that day. We were to open the house for the weekend. It was hot and still, so still at the Udebeck's that I thought I could hear Rapunzel's spinning wheel. The whole house spoke of secrets whispered in the sun-musty darkness of the rooms. I felt a curious sweet pull and was glad when mother said I didn't have to wear anything. I could just run around and practice Modern Health, but I was to stay in the back of the property where I was not likely to encounter any of the locals, old-fashioned folk who apparently didn't go in for Modern Health.

I dashed outside and right away found some raspberry bushes full of ripe berries. I sat down while stuffing my mouth so full it overflowed. I loved the sticky juice on my chest and belly. I dipped my forefinger into the sticky mess, stuck my belly out as far as I could and drew flower shapes on it. Then I remembered the river. It would be wonderful to jump into dark water and to feel with my toes if I could still reach the muddy river bed.

I ran to the dock and was about to throw myself into the

water when I saw something strange. My mother was sitting naked, spread-legged on the equally naked Uncle Walt, bouncing up and down, making sounds I thought only Oma Anna's needy women would make. She pulled on her hair, and then let herself fall on her hands so that she stood on all fours above Walt. Vomit rose in my throat. Were they killing each other? Without another thought I raced across the lawn toward them and threw myself under my mother's body, not an easy job since I had to both push and crawl. Walt sat up, wrapped his arms around both my mother and me and said: "You are both my girls." He was trying to calm my obvious fears, while my mother was furious. "Get into the house this minute and clean yourself," she said in the voice of the Snow Queen. "The others will be here in a minute."

I don't remember how I managed to spend the rest of the weekend, but my trust in Walt and my mother was shattered. Mathias sighed and shook his head. "I think that for a while you and Anna should go out to the Letzes on the weekends. You won't get into trouble there. By the way, I have to go away for a while. Take care of your Oma, and I'll see you as soon as I can. Remember: Go to your other grandparents." It was a piece of advice I gladly followed.

chapter eight
MY MOTHER THE BRIDE

Although spending time with my paternal grandparents, the Letzes, was part and parcel of our everyday life, it wasn't all that easy for me to follow Mathias' advice. How I spent time was strictly regulated by the adults around me and depended on their moods. In particular, I found my mother hard to manage. Despite our altercations, I was aware that she desperately needed to be thought of as a good mother. She made good this claim – so she thought – on two occasions when, in my absence, she correctly guessed that I had fallen ill. Both times she was sailing the Mediterranean with Walt, and the stories that got back to me were dramatic indeed. On one occasion, she woke from a nap and declared that she had to get back to Germany because I was ill. Nothing could stop her. She arrived in Berlin early in the morning, wild eyed and exhausted after having literally traveled all day and night. Hannibal could not have had as much trouble crossing the Alps with his elephants as my mother had rushing to my rescue.

She found me ill indeed. But Oma Anna and Opa Ferdinand were taking care of me, a doctor had been summoned, and I was busy recovering and, in the process, ruling my grandparents tyrannically. Oma Anna asked why mother hadn't called before she returned. (We took calls from the public phone at Helga's pub.) A telegram could have established contact. Mother flew into a rage. She had given up part of her vacation and here they were accusing her of not being a good mother!! Both grandparents were speechless.

Later, Mother used this incident to establish her reputation within the Udebeck family as an exquisitely sensitive wife and mother. I saw how many admired her false image, so much so that even I began to believe in a "Victoria Louise," as she called herself now, who had gone to the best private schools on scholarships because her father had died young and her mother was close to "passing" now. My mother exhorted me to mind my manners and forbade me to talk about Anna and Ferdinand.

Before he married my mother in May, 1941, the more liberal Walt sought to entertain guests Mother did not deem appropriate. She pointed out that certain people were simply not suitable for her soirees or for Walt's career. What she meant was that anyone who knew of her origins was banned from the house. I took this to mean that I, too, could be summarily dismissed and was kept around on probation, so to speak.

At times my skin crawled when Mother dropped a tidbit that revealed something about her ostensible background. When Cousin Adelheid and her preposterous, titled father came calling, the Count complained that the young folk no longer learned good French, even in the expensive private schools parents in "our circles" sent their children to. Mother, graciously offering black market cigars from Cuba, smiled her seductive best and said casually: "Yes, in my days at school a *jeune fille* was expected to know French very well. It was part of one's station in life." I no longer gulped when she took these little detours into a fictitious past. I had earned some hefty

Elaine's mother, Charlotte Resca Letz, in 1943,
some two years after her remarriage

Ohrfeigen (wallops on the ear) when I had spoken out in the presence of visitors. Her confabulations were necessary, she held, because of "the times." Her "castle in the clouds," as she liked to call it, needed a solid base in the here and now. Ferdinand and Helga's father had often discussed how this or that big Nazi "had feet of clay." So did my mother, though I was the only one to see them.

It was difficult to love my mother after I put all this information together. What could I do but grow up speedily so that I could go to America and find my father. These thoughts made me feel better. I even stopped feeling the volcanic anger that was slowly building inside me. I felt a gorgeous, thick, but cold kind of carapace grow around me, a kind of numb victory that allowed me to take everything in stride because I was now certain that I could build a life that was not controlled by Mother. I knew I would have to wait until I was older, but when I understood the manipulations the women in my life resorted to, I felt certain that I could play this game. However, I also knew that my mother was a formidable foe who would try to disgrace me – this I knew with certainty. I also knew that she would forever deny where she came from, flashing her expensive diamond ring.

The long-awaited wedding was a real disappointment. I had imagined a grand ballroom with crystal chandeliers, an orchestra playing waltzes, myself as somehow both flower girl and train bearer, my mother wearing a lovely white dress full of embroidery and, of course, the family jewels adorning her long neck. In the weeks leading up to the event, I had quizzed Mother Gräfchen exhaustively on the subject of weddings in the upper ranks of society, and we speculated on what my role in the wedding would be. I had high hopes that Mother Gräfchen and Mathias auf der Heyde would be invited. They were so much part of my life that I simply could not imagine significant family events without them. Besides, Mother Gräfchen claimed to have known my mother ever since, as a distraught preschooler, she had come to Berlin to live with the Schwagers. I was by now so used to my mother's stories and many attempts to obliterate the past that I did not blink an eyelid when Mother Gräfchen told me how hurt she had been when in the beginning of our relationship she was treated like a dangerous stranger by Mother. Suffice it to say, she received no wedding invitation.

On a foggy November morning, a slight drizzle polishing the streets a steel grey, a caravan of ten cars, each with a small bouquet of white carnations tied to its antenna, presented itself in front of the new apartment in which my mother and I had lived for the past two months. Uncle Walt would become "Dad" after the wedding, I was informed by Mother in her sternest tone. I had no intention of following that instruction. Grandmother Amanda's teachings and reminiscences of my American father's youth had indoctrinated me deeply. Nobody else could be either Dad or Father to me! When Mother asked if I would find it easier to call Walt "Dad" in English, I had a silent fit. She really knew how to humiliate a person.

The cars, all pearl grey Mercedes with oxblood-colored leather interiors, had a ghostly quality, their color deepening in the fine drizzle until they seemed to be one-dimensional reflections of themselves. The white carnations maintained their sprightliness even though the white satin ribbons that bound them had become soggy and seemed to hold them back from flight. The limousines were filled with elegant people, most of them unknown to me. Those to whom I had been introduced waved to me. My mother had rushed to the first car in an effort to preserve her designer dress. The door had been held open by Schloske, the chauffeur, who was holding an umbrella for her. But when I tried to follow my mother into the warm and dry interior of the car, he closed the door and waved me on. I didn't know which car had room for me. Walt's mother, soon to be my step-grandmother, sat majestically in the second car, obviously as distressed as I was. She called to her chauffeur who climbed out of his car and escorted me to the last one, whose driver was unknown to me. By now, soaking wet and angry, I stuck my tongue out at him. "Spoiled, arrogant brat" he hissed. But I had already learned well. "One more word out of you and I'll report you to my grandmother, my man, and do turn on the heat so I can dry off."

I had counted on being allowed to sit with Opa Ferdinand, but I hadn't seen him in any of the cars either. I felt a shock from my wet toes to my sodden hair. Wasn't he invited either? Instantly, I was sorry that I had not let the chauffeur know that I was really and truly a socialist who had landed among the rich folk through no fault of my own. The immediate need to become presentable in my wet dress overrode such concerns. I took it off carefully and instructed the driver to turn the heater fan as high as it would go. My mother had a cape that matched her dress, so she would be all right, I knew. But my new custom-made dress was made of silk; it dried rapidly but was totally wrinkled and puckered up in places. I slipped it on and wrapped the broad sash that went with it around my shoulders, letting it cascade down my front. I hadn't played dress-up with Mother Gräfchen and Oma Anna for nothing. I had portrayed maidens in distress dozens of times with both of them. Still, unwanted tears pressed against my eyes. Where was Oma Anna now and what was she doing?

The chapel where the wedding vows were to be exchanged lay in the distant periphery of Berlin. It seemed to take forever to get there. I had been told that the chapel had been built by an early Udebeck and was considered very special. All Udebecks got married there and a good many "slept their final sleep there," Walt's mother had explained.

Seated in the luxurious car as we travelled to my mother's wedding made me even more uncomfortable. Reminiscences spilled over the anger I felt about being treated like a second-class citizen, now with a thoroughly wet dress. Suddenly the motorcade came to a halt. A brass band met and serenaded us. The rain did not improve their performance. They sounded like drowned men with large air bubbles streaming out of their mouths.

While I was trying to figure out what was going on, Schloske appeared out of nowhere. He smiled and said: "Very different from the opera, what Miss?" After a brief conversation with my driver, he invited me to come with him. I was astonished because it turned out I had not been forgotten. Walt's mother, shortly to become "Grandmama," had used the time devoted to the welcoming brass band to rescue me and to right a couple of other mishaps. I hurriedly slipped into the vestry where a stout woman in the costume of the region was testing an old fashioned iron, the kind that is fed by an insert previously heated in the stove. "Quickly, Miss," she said and invited me to take my dress off so she could iron it. Walt's mother herself was there, her whole commanding presence apparently focused on two young men in Nazi uniforms.

I felt embarrassed and did not want to take off the wrinkled dress. At least it offered protection from the glances of the two men. They were receiving a harsh dressing down from Walt's mother. "Under no circumstances will you attend your cousin's wedding in those outfits," she coldly declared. "Gerda here has brought her husband's suits. There is no time to find you something else." The two demurred but did not get very far. One sputtered: "How does a divorced Jewess with a grown child fit into the family better than we do? We are the New Germany and the family will either have to get used to it or perish. Grandpapa would never have received her or her brat." "Perhaps not," Grandmama answered imperiously. "But at least she has good table manners and is willing to learn. That is more than one can say about that Austrian upstart. No manners at all."

While this exchange was going on I slipped back into my freshly ironed dress. The two young men had also changed and stood unhappily in the coarse Sunday best of Gerda's husband. Gerda curtsied in their direction. "If it pleases your Excellencies, I will keep your other clothes here until after the nuptials." She held the uniforms away from her body as though they were dangerous animals. Grandmama merely harrumphed and motioned to me to get back into the car. "This village, when it was still a village and not the prey of people with no names and no manners, it belonged to the first Udebeck," she muttered by way of explanation.

Then it dawned on me what a gigantic change my mother had effected. My heart beat so strongly that I thought it could be seen through the tight bodice of my dress. I didn't know whether I should confide in Grandmama how Helga and I felt about the Bum from Austria and allow myself to gloat at the momentary defeat of her two Nazi relatives. Or perhaps I should wait to talk to my mother to warn her about the Nazis who had infiltrated even the safe harbor of our new family. Or perhaps it would suffice simply to make sure that, here and now, in this strange new environment, she was still my mother. She certainly looked beautiful in her special dress, even though it didn't resemble a bridal gown at all. It clung to her so tightly in certain places that Opa Ferdinand and Grandmother Amanda would surely have found it indecent.

When I joined the procession to the dim altar, I heard the gasp that came from the guests when my mother entered the church on the arm of Uncle Walt. The chapel was damp and smelled moldy. Even the large flower arrangements looked as though they would shed moisture on the assembled group. Uncle Walt and Mother were quickly married without much fanfare. I heard the people behind me whisper about how unusual it was to have the groom give the bride to himself. "Just like Waldemar," an unknown informant told me. "Remember when he set off the helium balloons over Berlin and they thought it was a space boat?" "Yes," his neighbor recalled, "and what about that motorcycle he drove everywhere? I am surprised they came in decent cars today. I expected a motorcycle band."

Nobody made mention of my mother's family or noticed that I was there. I was again invisible. But a few surprises were still in store for me. As I sulked in a corner of the vestibule, a temporary receiving line was formed under the eagle eye of Walt's mother, now Grandmama. I was not included, but Oma Anna was there! I couldn't believe it. There she was in her Navy blue Sabbath dress with the lave collar and the gold star of David on a long gold chain around her neck. I tried to throw myself in her arms, but Opa Ferdinand stopped me. "The doctor only allowed her a few hours. She is full of medicines and can't take much excitement," he whispered in my ear. And, indeed, no sooner had the crowd thinned somewhat, than I saw Opa Ferdinand taking Oma Anna to a waiting car.

Neither was present at the ensuing dinner served in some relative's townhouse as the family regarded restaurants as vulgar. It was a quiet affair, but I heard the men say that the wine was "exquisite like the bride." There was chamber music, walls of flowers, some speeches, and two male servants in frock coats and white gloves. Telegrams were read from relatives and friends who could not attend. They included congratulations from the family of the deposed Prime Minister and from the English and Danish branches of the family.

Amid all of this splendor, everybody appeared subdued. There was much talk about the possibility of war. The two Nazi cousins comported themselves like public orators until some of the older men told them, "Enough." But their enthusiasm for Hitler had effectively undone the atmosphere that had just begun to be festive.

My mother was oblivious to it all. She had achieved what she set out to do and thoroughly enjoyed her success. I noticed that she drank more wine than I had ever seen her consume before. I soon became tired of sitting at the long table, forced to answer politely the few questions that came my way. One course followed another, each one so beautifully garnished that it appeared to be a still life. One had to eat quickly though, because as new courses were being served, the earlier ones were simultaneously swept away. The rhythm was determined by the speed with which the newlyweds ate. It provided a lesson that I would fall back on many times in the future.

I was to suffer from this bit of "good manners" on many other occasions. Without saying so, the Udebecks expected the "young people" to fall in line and practice the kind of courtesies associated with life at the many aristocratic homes scattered throughout Germany. I gathered that in the Udebeck clan even the deposed Kaiser Wilhelm II, now living in Holland, was considered a "freethinker" who did not conform to their vision of feudal hierarchy. Their view of the world had gotten stuck around 1860 when Count Bismarck held sway. Even now, the Udebecks were not sure if health insurance for workers, accident insurance, and pensions for the elderly – all instituted by the Iron Chancellor – were good things.

At the wedding, I heard some Junkers who were great landowners in East Prussia complain that "the peasantry had been spoiled for two generations by these social measures and were not willing to work diligently on the land, as they had done for ages before." "They were free now after all," a second *Gutsherr* (landowner) commented. Nobody was a serf anymore, but these "ungrateful wretches" were incapable of feeling committed to the families whose land they were tending.

The two men heaved a sigh. One of them, the Count, noticed me and pulled me closer. "So you are the young filly who has infiltrated the family. Let me look at you." He placed his hands on my shoulders and eyed me critically. I held my breath, hoping he would stop staring at me. His companion turned away as though told to do so. "Well cousin," he breathed softly, suddenly displaying a smile I didn't like at all. I was standing in a corner, close to the sideboard. He pressed his huge body against me and groped for my small breasts. "Ho, not quite there yet, are we," he breathed even harder. "You'll be delicious in another year."

Despite myself I felt tears gathering in my eyes. I remembered the salesman on the pier off the North Sea resort against whom I had defended my mother. Could I do any less for myself? I balled my fists and struck as hard as I could in the confined space, landing blows on his soft gut. Unprepared for such resistance, he let go of me long enough to permit my escape. My mother had noticed something and came over to see what the turmoil was all about. I knew that she was on pins and needles lest her few family members disgrace her. "Are you minding your manners?" she asked with a smile. "Sure she is," the Count said. "Charming child. We've been making friends."

Just as I was about to tell my mother the truth he got hold of my shoulder again and squeezed so hard I couldn't get a word out. Whether my mother noticed anything I'll never know, but she took my hand and said, "Come and meet some of your other new cousins." I was safe then and glad to meet other members of the family. Among others, I was introduced to Cousin Adelheid, the pederast Count's daughter. She blushed deeply, and I wondered if she knew about her father's escapades. She was said to spend all of her time riding or taking care of her horses. She immediately invited me to visit her and her father at their estate in East Prussia, though there were a good 15 years between us. Cousin Jorgen later informed me that Adelheid was lonesome and would invite anyone to visit who could walk upright.

Some older ladies tried to engage me in conversation too. "And where did you say you went to school, dear?" asked several of them, who then shook their heads when I told them. "They really have to take her out of those proletarian schools," one of them said loud enough for me to hear. "She'll have a hard enough time fitting in without a school reinforcing the vulgarities she has lived with." I thought she meant the times I had to leave the classroom when the Nazi party group leaders came to give "political science classes," or when I had to stand in the back of the class when the music teacher taught patriotic songs.

As though all this wasn't enough excitement for one evening, Uncle Walt had another surprise in store for me. He and mother planned a trip to Norway for their honeymoon. I assumed that I would stay at the apartment as usual. But no, this was not the plan. After dinner, I was told that I had not been informed of the changes because my mother "feared my temper." It seemed that Oma Amanda had been asked to take me in for two weeks. I was not to be alone in the apartment, where the staff would be joining the cook in the days ahead. Grandmama was to preside over them all but go home at night. I was considered too much of a handful for her and it was feared that I would fall prey to my presumed *Drang nach unten* (urge to join the lower classes) if I were to stay home alone with the servants. So Oma Amanda would take care of me while her son's ex-wife was on her honeymoon with her new husband. Even I could see how bizarre this arrangement was. But I looked forward to staying with the Letzes, despite the long tram ride to and from school.

chapter nine
THE LETZES' GARDEN

I had many misgivings about my mother's decision to marry a second time. It wasn't so much that I felt loyalty to my father, though I told myself that this must be the source of my discomfort. There was no one with whom I could discuss my problems. The reliable Helga was far away, and my former home was on the other side of Berlin. My mother cited a sudden lack of funds as the reason I should not use the phone. When I asked Walt whether we had suddenly become poor, he smiled his enigmatic smile and muttered something about the wedding having cost more than anticipated. At Oma Amanda's I never had to worry about what fork I used or how I addressed her friends. I was not excluded from adult conversations. Quite the contrary, I became the center of attention when Amanda sailed importantly into the second court of the tenement where she had lived for all of her married life.

On arrival late in the afternoon, some of the men were already home from work. Two or three hastily dropped their whittling and the newspaper they shared. They were all ready to take my fairly heavy suitcase upstairs for us. One of them, Herr Hubler, wanted to carry my short grandmother, too. I could see this was a standard joke Herr Hubler played with quite proper Oma Amanda. She blushed like a young girl and insisted he put her down. "And see that you confess this to that priest of yours," she snapped at him.

He was an immediate source of fascination for me. I only knew Protestants and Jews. Mother Gräfchen and her church had remained separate from any denomination in my head, more like a Shangri La or the Garden of Eden. Herr Hubler descended on me and offered to carry me instead of Oma Amanda. Before I could say anything in my own defense, Amanda was on him like a wild cat. He covered his face and retreated while the other men laughed. "There he goes, big Nazi jerk," Herr Musikonate said loudly enough for Hubler to hear. "He is the biggest Red around here, but today he wipes his ass exclusively with the swastika."

My grandmother became incensed. "In front of the child we don't talk like that, Musiko, as a matter of fact, we never talk like that to anyone. Mr. Letz would have your head if he knew how you talk in front of his wife and his granddaughter." With a haughty look she grabbed my hand and pulled me away from the laughing men. "I wish we could move away from these barbarians," she sighed. "But everything is so expensive."

Nevertheless, being at Oma Amanda's and Opa Christian's was calming. I felt for the first time in a long while that I was appreciated and that it was perfectly all right to be myself. I felt quite flattered when some of the ladies from Oma's church showed up to "view" me. Oma explained that when a new person joined her church or when a baby was born, certain members formed a committee and went to view the new addition. Obviously, I fit into neither category, and Oma laughed. "They are religious and true believers, but many of them can barely read and write. Because they cannot read they are doubly nosy for anything out of the ordinary, but they are also ashamed for being nosy. So they formed the committee in order to find out what you are like." She chuckled so long that Opa Christian finally asked what was so funny. Oma hugged me and stroked my hair. "They don't know that she is really just my granddaughter whom I love." I was grateful not only for her affection but the fact that she didn't attach a qualifier to her love – a qualifier like "even though she is half Jewish" or "but she goes to a hoity-toity school now and isn't really one of us anymore."

The ladies of the committee arrived punctually and were served coffee and home-baked cake. They obviously enjoyed their repast, even though it was only 9:30 a.m., hardly the time one usually has whipped cream on multi-layered tarts. They all had ice-cold hands, high, quavering voices, and smelled of mothballs. Of course they had to sing a few hymns and pray before "viewing" me. Oma Amanda ran around serving everyone strong coffee in her China set, her *Sammeltassen*. She was very proud of her collection of fine china cups. It was one of the joys of her life, and she knew all the major manufacturers, the locations of factories, the quality ratings, and sometimes even the names of the pattern designers. Opa Christian hid himself in the only other room of the apartment. "They might want to 'view' me too – in my coffin," he whispered as he closed the door.

Oma Amanda had stationed me at the apartment door and instructed me to greet each visitor with a handclasp. "No curtsy?" I inquired. Oma gave me a stern look. "No affected monkey shines here," she said. But Walt's mother, now Grandmama, had already gotten hold of my imagination and my behavior. I automatically curtsied as each woman puffed herself up the stairs, leaned gasping on the banister, and bade me summon "Sister." Much to my amazement, "Sister" turned out to be my grandmother. What a dried up bunch, I thought.

They were evenly divided about whether my behavior was

merely old-fashioned or purposely designed to make them aware of their lower station in life. I could see Grandmother Amanda gloating a bit about so much attention being paid to me and my way of presenting myself when actually this was a Sunday morning prayer session with a simple "viewing" tacked on to the end. The committee members were not part of this prayer group. I also noted that my grandmother seemed to hold a position of respect in the mainly female gathering. One old lady, smelling of peppermint and alcohol, gushed: "Sister Letz is our darling angel helper when one of us passes to the Beyond. She knows so much about loss."

At first I thought the old lady meant my ever-absent and yet ever-present father in America, but when I looked at Oma Amanda's face I knew Hildchen was meant, the child Oma had lost to diphtheria so many years ago. Every once in a while, when she encouraged me to help her with household tasks, such as putting away freshly ironed linens or dusting books and knickknacks, we would come across an incomplete knitting or a notebook, sometimes even what looked like a rag but was actually a piece of child's underwear that had escaped Oma's insatiable need to iron and smooth whatever she came across. On such occasions, she would sigh and take the found object from me rather brusquely, exclaiming "that is one of Hildchen's." Apparently, I was not to touch the stuff, even as she remarked that Hildchen had accompanied her and learned how to keep house at her side just as I was doing now. Out of her prolonged mourning had grown a reputation as a staunch helper in times of crisis, including death. If a child was hurt or a husband fell desperately ill, Oma Amanda was called by the members of her church and her tenement neighbors before the doctor, or more ominously, the clergyman and undertaker.

Opa Christian was opposed to her involvement with the sorrow of so many others. "She won't let Hildchen rest," he would mutter. It now dawned on me that Oma Amanda always wore black, something I had never thought about. Once she had remarked that many women wore such dark clothes because they showed less dirt and, with the addition of a jacket or shawl, one looked good enough to do the daily food shopping. But that is not what motivated Oma Amanda. For her, the black dress showed that she was still in mourning. I thought it all creepy and preferred not to think about it. For me, the Letzes had always been, and still were, a second safe haven. I didn't want them to have problems or to live by a code of rules I didn't understand.

Despite Amanda's growing discomfort, Frau Lehrmann continued her paean of praise. "It is horrible to lose a child, but Sister knew where to find help," she simpered while digging into the delicious cake. "Because of Hildchen, your grandmother learned to take care of the dying. She had her spiritual homecoming when Hildchen went to heaven." Here, finally, was part of an answer to a puzzle that had long plagued me. Why had my grandparents Letz not stayed with the Lutherans, the group they had been born into and to whom the majority of people around us belonged?

Through tears, Amanda clarified this matter for me. "It wasn't only because of Hildchen," she began. "How could I stay with a religious group that thinks of the Jew-hating Hitler as a savior when my own grandchild is part Jew? No, that could not be. So Christian and I decided to do some good in the world, to help raise you and to see what we could do for the black children of Africa." She showed me one of the missionary magazines I frequently read in her home. There were pictures of children with huge bellies, runny noses, and infected eyes. Few of them had clothes on. Everyone else had fallen respectfully silent, but no one approached my grandmother to comfort her. With a lump in my throat, I put my arms around her.

When I helped Oma wrap pieces of cake for those who could not come to our meeting but were eager to hear about it, she had nothing but praise for me and my behavior. She positively glowed. I was totally amazed at my social success. I was so accustomed to hearing how ill-mannered and stubborn I was that I was ready to join any group in which I could exonerate myself, even this one. But of course I knew that my mother would not permit it. I knew full well that this visit was a special occasion and that in the future I would see very little of the Letzes.

The two sides of my family had long opposed one other on the question of my religious upbringing. Oma Amanda saw it as the "life of her soul," whereas Oma Anna just smiled and waved her hand to indicate mild disapproval of such an extravagant claim. Because I would not let up with my questions, a compromise was reached: I would be allowed to attend a Catholic Church service. "At least they will have some decent artwork there," Mother observed. "Show her the statuary and there might be some good paintings of the Madonna, by second-tier artists, of course. In this Protestant country, they don't spend the money on churches like they do in the Latin countries. If the child shows any interest in the pictures or statues, we'll take her to the museums."

Oma Anna was shocked. "That is not how one teaches about religion. And since when have you been an art critic? I thought we were talking of the child being exposed to religion. Or maybe you don't need such a thing in America?" They talked as though I weren't in the room with them. And why were they always mentioning America? I was fairly sure we would not go back there because of what Opa Ferdinand had said. Both he and Anna both thought my father, Fred Letz, a bum, a judgment I always hid from Amanda, who remained quite fond of her son.

On Saturday afternoons, Oma Anna, Opa Ferdinand and I liked to go to their *Schrebergarten* because Amanda always had wonderful cake and whipped cream for anyone who showed up. And there were many, indeed. As with many other private initiatives, the stream of participants had dwindled tremendously since Hitler's grasp on the country had tightened. There were only a few old folks who still came, ate their cake, and mumbled the obligatory prayers. Then, as goods became sparse during the war years, Amanda and Christian fed many again, often being the only providers of food for whole families. We, however, brought our own supper of cold cuts and potato or cucumber salad with us in order to avoid being a further strain on the Letzes' budget.

Anna was very fond of Amanda's garden and I knew that the two couples would have been close friends if not for the trouble between my mother and my American father. The Letzes' vegetable patch was located amid a colony of small, illegal sheds that some families actually made their homes. Others, like my grandparents, leased the plot of land from the city to grow flowers and vegetables, the purpose for which the *Schrebergarten* were intended. These green areas were the invention of the physician Dr. Daniel Gottlieb Moritz Schreber, who dedicated his life to the harmonious interaction of school and home, physical culture and manual work. He gained a lasting reputation as the founder of therapeutic gymnastics. It was not known at the time that this same Schreber Senior was a fanatic and a bully, and that his withholding of affection most certainly led to the mental breakdown of his son when the latter was president of the high court of Dresden.

Opa Christian, my paternal grandfather, had a reputation for being a super gardener. He knew how to graft espalier fruit and regularly harvested plums, cherries, and apples. He and Oma Amanda were revered by many because they not only provided canned fruits and vegetables to their extended family and friends but also to all sorts of needy persons. Naturally, my mother scoffed at them and their charitable works. "Imagine belonging to a sect that has no structure, just wants to do good, and prays all the time. I won't let the child go there if they fill her head with those silly sayings of theirs."

"Don't be absurd," Oma Anna replied. "That's lots better than what she hears in school from those Nazis." "Not for much longer," mother triumphantly replied. "Soon we'll all be out of this mess and you, Mother, must dress better and stop wearing those hideous aprons." Oma Anna and I had just come home from helping Oma Amanda pit a slew of cherries to be put up for dessert in winter. We looked a mess, all right, with cherry juice all over us. I wore twin cherry earrings. We felt good about our work and about ourselves and didn't need mother to spoil it all. Just to annoy her, I asked to be taken to the Letzes' religious services.

I remembered that I had been taken there once, but that my mother had forbidden more visits. But I kept insisting, so Oma Anna finally relented and let me go with them to "their sect." I encountered a group of sweaty people in dark clothing singing enthusiastically until one of them got up and read from the Bible. Then another followed, and everyone shouted "Amen!" for reasons I could not understand. I did find one of their publications in the ladie's room and discovered that the sect was doing missionary work in East Africa, trying to establish schools there as well as in Berlin. My paternal grandparents belonged to a group of elders who shared their "relative wealth," which, in their case, meant their homegrown fruits and vegetables.

Opa Christian was not the praying type, as he said, but he did believe in helping people. He created a wonderful orchard in which he performed such miracles as grafting small apricot twigs into pear espaliers. He carefully wrapped sticky bandages around the cuts and nurtured the trees like babies. Of course he made the wooden trellises himself. When Oma Amanda and I first saw the small golden yellow pears held tightly by their part of the lattice work accompanied by tiny velvety apricots, we cried. Opa Christian shook his head: "Women!" he complained. "And now you will tell me that you are crying because you are happy!" "But we are, Christian," Oma Amanda wiped her eyes. "You've built what was best about your folks' farm right here."

In fact, Opa Christian's family did not approve of Amanda. She was not a suitable farm wife with her fancy lace tablecloths, her tiny figure, and her refusal to speak the local dialect. "German is a beautiful language. Let's keep it at that," she would haughtily remark when the country folk came to visit, hoping to hasten their return to the farm.

Despite their differences Amanda and Christian had important things in common. When each had completed the eighth grade their fathers took them aside and said: "Now that you are old enough to make your own way in the world, don't let anyone know you belong here if you get into trouble. But tell everyone to whom you belong when you succeed." My great grandfathers felt they had done well by their offspring. The government was lax about school attendance, and school only consisted of six mandatory grades. Thus, Amanda and Christian were privileged young people with just enough education for a good start in life. Christian was apprenticed to a butcher, while his older brother was to inherit the farm. But he lasted only three months with the butcher and then ran away.

Christian found a job with the streetcar services of the Municipality of Berlin. It was his first job and would remain his only one. But he not only found a job, he also found Amanda, who had become a parlor maid. She had certain privileges that other servants did not have because the lady of the house was a very distant relative. There was also a silent pact with her parents that this lady would look for a husband for Amanda. After all, she was almost a housekeeper, permitted to give out the linens to housemaids and the tablecloths to the man servant who waited table. Amanda told us many times and with great relish how she was given the keys to the wine cellar and was taught to choose, uncork, and pour wines. The man servant had been caught once too often selling the master's stores though, much to Amanda's chagrin, he was not sacked.

Amanda met Christian at the time she was stewing over this incident. On their halfday off they were sitting in a pleasant open air coffee house on the outskirts of Berlin, she drinking coffee with a daintily raised pinky finger, he drinking a huge stein of beer which, as it turned out, he did not even enjoy but thought it manly to imbibe. When Amanda repeatedly blew her nose with indignation, Christian introduced himself. "She sounded like a grey goose setting out for warm climates in the fall," he commented wryly. According to Amanda, he looked fetching in his black conductor's uniform. "It was love at first sight," she told us, blushing like the young thing she had been.

Her heart pounding because she was allowing herself to be picked up by a stranger, she pulled herself up to her full five feet one and gave him her name, adding daughter of Paulus Tedke, chief of police in Tiefburg-am-Blitzen." She was hoping the addendum would keep the handsome young man respectful, a fact Christian never failed to mention when the story was retold. "I knew right away then that I would have to stand at attention for the rest of my life. Mandy was a stickler for correctness even then." Having recounted their budding romance he would either put his arm around her shoulders or pick her up, enjoying her laughing, kicking complaints. Inevitably came the injunction I knew so well: "Not in front of the child."

I was mighty tired of being a child but nobody seemed to notice. I was placed into the advanced Sunday school class where I soon garnered the reputation of a fierce debater of Talmud, Torah, and New Testament. Nobody thought to ask me how and where I acquired my knowledge. Actually, it was gleaned from the soft old prayer books Opa Christian found in the dump near their *Schrebergarten*. I also found Books of Commentary and a Bible hidden in Oma Anna's wardrobe. When I felt ill-understood and was angry, I repaired into those breathless quarters with a flashlight and brooded in anticipation of my Jehovah-like revenge.

The shabby lives of my Grandmother Amanda's group of devotees repelled me. I had a sneaking suspicion that they were part of the non-Aryan group Hitler wanted to get rid of. Their sparse, worn clothing and unwashed armpits elicited no compassion from me. As a matter of fact, I began to accept their shy homage as my due. One pudgy woman, accompanied by a sturdy SA trooper, began to cry when she saw me. Dousing me with bad breath that reeked of years of dental neglect, she pawed me until I stiffened and tried to pull back.

At this, everyone became markedly uncomfortable; only old Mrs. Lehrmann remained at ease. The crying woman was not only her daughter, it turned out, but also the mother of my recently deceased friend, Margot. Margottchen's mother had become a respectable married lady "thanks to *der Führer*," Mrs. Lehrmann proudly announced. Apparently she had undergone job training and was now employed as matron in a home for foreign women who either came to Germany of their own free will or had been pressed into service by their new German masters. Everyone was interested in the details, but not until a greeting ritual of some magnitude had been performed. Margottchen's mother went from one to the other in order to shake hands and to introduce herself to those she didn't know. Very close in back of her, the SA man stood at attention, snapped his heels together, and gave the Hitler salute. I could not help but giggle, though Oma Amanda threw me a warning look.

The gathering fell apart soon after the arrival of Margottchen's mother and her SA trooper; nor did they stay long. Neither Oma nor Opa welcomed them; indeed, I had never seen them so cold toward fellow human beings. Opa Christian murmured under his breath: "Damn the *Dreckskerl* (bullshitter)." After the unwelcome couple had finally left, without the customary gift of a piece of a cake or some fruit from Oma, he explained: "That guy has been looking for a handout since the day he was born. First, he was a holy Royalist, nothing but the

Kaiser would do for him as long as those dumb aristocrats lent him money and let him sleep in their stables or garages. He came from my village, I know him. Then, the Communists gave him better food and let him sleep in their district office. And now, of course, he fits right in with the Nazi set-up. He's a bad one who doesn't mind telling lies about people to the Nazis for the price of a glass of beer."

I soon forgot about this unhappy outing because of Oma Amanda's idea. On the next Sunday, my last one at her house, we would go to see Oma Anna at the sanitarium. We got up very early on the appointed day, so early that the flower vendors and the bakers were not even about. We first took the tram to a commuter railroad that took us past suburbs like Steglitz and Grunewald to Potsdam. At Potsdam (where it was being rumored I might be sent to school) we took a regular train to Brandenburg. By the time we arrived and walked into the sanitarium we were both exhausted.

The facility turned out to be a pleasant enough building set in a huge garden that was populated by all sorts of people, some of them engaged in animated conversations with themselves. We rang a bell, were admitted, and were then brought to a large, light room where Anna was sitting on a bench with several other women. She was teaching them how to knit her special pattern. When she saw us, she dropped her knitting and limped rapidly toward us, her arms outstretched and her face – oh, her face! She was radiant, and her joy at seeing us spread to the others who also began to smile at us. At which point a hefty nurse appeared. "And how old is the Fräulein?" she asked. "Why, 12," Oma Amanda and I said at the same time. I was taller than she by then and was beginning to develop. I often felt clumsy next to my tiny, fine-boned grandmother. The nurse said "Well, I surely thought the Fräulein was 14, the minimum age by which we admit visitors. *Der Führer* feels what children might see here could frighten them."

Anna heard what was said, and her face became blank. Her

arms fell listlessly to her side. "That is my granddaughter," she almost whispered. "She is more mature than many an adult I know." The nurse took pity on us all and showed us a window from which Anna could wave to us. We stayed for half an hour, waving and shouting. I picked a few weeds with flowers that grew among the dusty curbstones and tried to throw them up to Anna, but they never reached her. She cried and closed the window.

I felt terribly ashamed. How could two grown women like my grandmothers allow themselves to cry in public? Didn't they know that in the New Germany all weakness was forbidden? I felt a cold chill between my shoulder blades. Suppose someone was watching us. They might call us degenerate weaklings and perhaps resettle us somewhere. Wouldn't our open display of emotions make things worse for Anna? Really, I thought, my new Grandmama, with her rigid adherence to protocol and manners, had something to offer that could make me stronger. By staying within her rules and regulations one could stay hidden in plain sight.

This very strategy had served me well during one night in particular. It was when Walt and Mother were not yet married, and I was still living with Oma Anna, who by then was beginning to act strangely. From the window in the living room we saw the local SA *Staffel* (Nazi Troops) emerging out of all sorts of nooks and crannies. Anna and I both exclaimed in astonishment when we realized how many of our neighbors were already in thrall of *Der Führer* and his insane ideology. The men outside all carried torches and seemed happily excited.

I found the flickering light and milling men exciting. Some women seemed to be joining the fray and were exhorting the men to fulfill whatever task lay ahead of them. I leaned further out the window to see and hear exactly what was going on, but as I strained to see, Oma suddenly grabbed me and pulled me roughly into the darkened room. She quickly shoved me under Opa Ferdinand's desk and, when I protested, she told me to be quiet. She herself crouched down near the window and from that awkward position reached up and closed it. "Maybe they'll forget we are here. Just be quiet, not a word out of you," she hissed. When I protested again, she shoved a blanket and some candy into my nest, then rammed Ferdinand's chair against the opening.

I understood that she was hiding me, but I was not at all certain that the upheaval in the street held any threat to us personally. I had to grow up before I understood that I had lived through the *Kristallnacht*, the "Night of Broken Glass." Oma Anna became caught up in memories of pogroms; she began talking about a brother Ernstle who had been lynched one Easter by a mob of Poles who had come across the border to avenge children who had supposedly been killed to make matzos. Soon Ferdinand came home from work. He was subdued as well. He had been in touch with my mother who told him that we were to go to the house of Walt's mother – not yet my Grandmama – in Grunewald.

Oma Anna wouldn't budge. "They are sure to need me here, with all those vandals loose. When they get going who knows what will happen. You take the child over to Walt Udebeck's mother and pray they don't stop you. And don't take the subway or the tram but do take your passport and the child's birth certificate."

She pulled me out of my nest and pushed me at Ferdinand. "I wish the child had an identity card, like everyone else. They wouldn't bother an American citizen." Opa grumbled, "I feel like a criminal smuggling her out of prison or something."

"She'll end up in a worse place than prison," Anna replied. "Her mother can't register her because then the *Rassenpolizei* [police department for racial purity] would definitely investigate her *Stammbaum* [genealogy] and we'd have to give her to her American father."

"I wonder if you aren't exaggerating," Ferdinand said. "What would they want with a little girl?"

Anna had had enough. She rammed her fists on her hips and shouted, "Where have you been all this time? Can't you see what's going on? Every bum and anti-Semite is out to get their share of the booty tonight." With this, the exchange ended, and Ferdinand took me to the home of my future Grandmama. And there I had my first lesson about how to be present without being seen.

The old lady was waiting for us but, atypically, no servant was to be seen. I had expected to find her sitting in her chair near the fireplace, drinking sherry and ready to give me one of her frequent lectures on how to behave "among civilized people." Instead, she had Ferdinand leave at once with warnings to stay away from public transportation, as a good many people had apparently been beaten on buses and trams. She allowed Ferdinand to use a bicycle belonging to her maid. No sooner had he left than there was a very loud knock on the door.

"You will answer," she told me. "But do not say one word. I will do the talking." My heart was beating so hard I was almost unable to breathe, and my legs were shaking. "Go, go," she pushed me toward the hall and the door. "Let me see some of that fire you are famous for."

I pulled myself together and opened the door. Sure enough, there stood a huge soldier, followed by three or four men in Nazi uniform. *N'abend* (good evening), he said. "Is the lady of the house in?" I nodded and opened the door wider. They all stormed in, nearly knocking me over. "Careful," the soldier shouted. He went to the open door to the living room, brought his heels together smartly, and bowed so deeply I thought he would surely fall down. Grandmama waved him in graciously. "Close the door, will you?" she said in my direction. I understood immediately that I was not to be seen or heard from.

I went to the library that opened into the living room and into the hall. There I sat down on the steps with wheels used to reach books on the higher shelves. I could see that the Nazis were looking around, though they did not turn the light on. They conferred with each other and pointed to some of the vases and pictures that were displayed. One of them spied me and came over. "What are you doing?" he asked. "Do you work here?" I felt inspired. "*Der Führer* does not permit children to work," I said with as much conviction as I could muster. The man backed off and went to his colleagues.

Shortly thereafter the whole group left. Grandmama told me that the officer had turned out to be someone who had been at university with one of her nephews and was ashamed to have to come to search her house for Jews. "He knew we wouldn't have any here," she said. I felt heat spreading through my body and wanted to lie down on the floor and kick and scream as I had done as a baby. I knew with absolute certainty that there was no such thing as a safe place for people like me.

Grandmama just wanted to keep her household safe, even if it meant putting up with a kid like me. "Go to the kitchen and tell the cook to give you something to eat," she instructed me. But the cook had been sent to bed. So I cut some bread, smeared some jam on it, and waited for morning to come. Nobody checked on me. Alone I survived a bitter night.

10.

chapter ten
MOTHER'S DREAM COME TRUE

When we said "goodbye" to each other after Walt and Mother had returned from their wedding trip, Oma Amanda and Opa Christian knew as well as I did that we would not see each other very often from now on, and when we did it would be on entirely different terms. But we said nothing of this to each other. They both hugged me and Oma pressed a 50RM bill into my hand. I put it down on the table. "Thanks, Oma, but I really can't take this from you."

Opa shoved me out into the hall. "Let her call you on the phone, okay? You are all she has left, what with Hildchen in her grave and your father in America." I hastily ran down the stairs and nearly dropped my suitcase when somebody grabbed me. "Take it easy, Miss." It was Schloske. I was pleased to see him. "Why didn't you tell me you would pick me up?" I wanted to know.

"I didn't know until this morning that I would have time. Sir left for Hamburg this morning, so Madame, your mother, sent me to fetch you."

The men who always hung around the large entry door of the tenement looked askance at us. To their eyes, it seemed outrageous that a grown man was catering to a child. They accepted that I belonged to one of the families living there. But they could not accept Schloske in his uniform, carrying my suitcase; the scene illustrated all that frustrated them in their own lives. One of them said: "Instead of that monkey suit you should be wearing the brown shirt. A grown man making believe he's working, playing with dolls." Another group stood at attention and made rude noises. Two of them, supposedly my grandparents' friends, started to goose step, shout *Heil Hitler,* give the Nazi salute, and make derogatory remarks.

Schloske became more upright than usual. "You're spending your energy in the wrong places, *Kumpels* (buddies)," he told the clowning men, every bit as aloof as his employers. Retribution followed immediately with the shout of "Jew lover. Whose ass do you have to lick in order to be kosher like your bosses?" Schloske pushed me into the car, locked the doors, and revved up the engine. We almost ran down one of the "clowns" who had tried to stop and provoke us. "You are very brave Schloske," I ventured. "Just following Sir's orders, Miss," he replied. I had become "Miss" instead of "the child" or "the girl" to Schloske. Apparently this had to do with my new status as the daughter of the house.

I actually liked the set-up. I had a large room all to myself and was required to perform only a few chores. I began to see why my mother had insisted on my learning "manners." In my former surroundings those few girls who were taught to curtsy on greeting grown-ups were expected to give up this practice when they started school. After age six or so it was no longer thought "cute." In my new household, however, I had to curtsy so often that I felt in danger of becoming lopsided. Fortunately, I only had to perform this onerous rite when ladies visited.

And how they visited! It seemed as though the Udebecks

were related to every noble family in Prussia, Pomerania, Brandenburg, and beyond. It was expected that the newlyweds would make an appearance at each household to which there were ties, and then a return visit had to take place. Understandably, the ladies wanted to see how we lived, which of the wedding presents were in use, and how I fit into the picture. It was bad enough that Mother was a commoner, but a divorcée with a child was beyond the pale. "If that isn't just like Walt. He always had a bent toward the exotic. Even as a child." They seemed either not to know or to disregard the awkward fact that we were Jewish.

I learned from some of his cousins that my new stepfather, when still a student, had threatened to marry the daughter of a Japanese man who was highly placed in the Japanese Embassy. The members of the family who had met her were beside themselves. She was not at all what they had anticipated. They had expected a shy fragile "Madame Butterfly blossom of a girl." Instead they met a *Burschikos* (a tomboy) who thought nothing of riding on the backseat of Walt's motor cycle. Cousin Adelheid, who was a regular visitor, confided, "She didn't even own a kimono."

Another time he and his fellow students filled balloons with a mixture of hydrogen and helium and let them burn in the night sky of Berlin. It was reported that he still smiled when reminded of this "joke." What thrilled him was that the incident was taken seriously and reported in the *Berliner Tagesblatt* (Berlin Daily) as some kind of astronomical anomaly. The tabloids made an even bigger deal out of the incident, interpreting it as the *Auftakt* (prelude) to Hitler's emergent power.

When reminded of this incident, Walt would mumble, "Shows you he is full of hot air." "You are going to have us all thrown in jail," the two young Hitler adherents I had met at the wedding admonished him. Walt grinned. "There are far too many of us. If they arrested the family, they would have to let the political prisoners go." "At least think of our careers," Cousin Guido begged. "How are Luigi and I going to get any place if you, our godfather, makes fun of *Der Führer*? It's bad enough that mother gave us those Italian names. By the way, we applied to change them. As soon as the papers come through we will be Heinrich and Ludwig."

Dad did not think this was funny. In fact, he forbade Guido and Luigi from coming to the house if they really planned to discard the names their mother gave them. She is, he added "a lovely, sensitive woman." As it turned out, we did not see Guido and Luigi again. We first read in the *Tagesblatt* that they had indeed given up their "heathenish" names, and then later learned they had suffered a *Heldentod* (hero's death) on the Western front.

Another story I heard repeatedly was of Walt's political activities. Over and over the visiting ladies assured my mother that Walt was really on the side of the monarchy. The proof resided in the fact that during a general strike he was among the volunteers who kept the trams, trains, buses and all manner of government establishments going. "Without the students' help, the good, honest members of the Proletariat would not have been able to go to work," Countess Hellerwinkel related with almost religious fervor. She was reported to have been in love with Walt since childhood, when he had found her in an old wardrobe stored in the attic. During a hide-and-go-seek game she had accidentally locked herself in. By the time Walt found her, she had a sore throat from screaming for a long time.

"I could only croak like a frog when he found me. I was soaking wet. The temperature inside that old thing must have been 100, and, of course I was petrified thinking that no one would find me and that I would have to die in there. It is almost comforting to think that someone of a future generation would find my little skeleton, all crunched down in the corner of this magnificent coffin." She waved a perfumed silk handkerchief until the room seemed permeated with its odors.

Walt was annoyed when Mother later recurred to the incident. "I wish the woman would keep her mouth shut," he exclaimed angrily. "I was never in love with her – even when we were children – and I certainly was not enamored of the lower classes, even though I am in favor of higher wages and a shorter work week. And she is still stuck on smell, always waving her perfume around. When we were children and I found her in the attic, she – excuse me, my dear – stank of sweat. Fear, I suppose. I told her so. And now she wafts smells at me and my family every chance she gets. Next we know she'll take Charlotte to pick out a perfume." He kissed my mother's hand.

"You are not gallant, dear," she smiled. "Imagine caring about someone for 20 years and never getting anything for your pains." I saw once more how enthralled Walt was with my mother. I almost came forward out of my corner to warn him about her. Mother clearly wanted something extraordinary from him, otherwise she would not have been so *trés gentile* about the other woman's tale and would have addressed the possessiveness underlying her rival's behavior. She generally did not allow anyone to show any allegiance, love, or admiration for Walt. She herself was the one person in his life permitted emotional contact with him, and she saw herself as the purveyor of all good things for him, erecting a wall between him and the world. I was no exception. I was beginning to see that I would get caught in Mother's web as well if I did not watch out. So Walt would have to be without warning from a stepdaughter who already owed him a great deal. When I wasn't busy shielding myself from mother's shifting temper, I could actually enjoy my new life.

I finally decided to be "good," to be whatever Mother wanted. Everyone around me was delighted with my change in behavior. Nobody recognized that I was acting like a general deploying his troops. I very much wanted to be with my mother. My two grandmothers loved me, true, but they were not "regular." Both sets of grandparents had their own agendas; I was thrown in as a bonus, or so it seemed. While Oma Anna and Opa Ferdinand were busily trying to change their world through political activity, grandparents Letz strove to maintain their own small world, growing fruit and giving it away to those around them.

"Being good" was part and parcel of my defense against my mother's passionate and sometimes unreasonable demands. At least, there was a sort of cease-fire between us that was reinforced by Mother's more cordial relations with me. I no longer lived in close proximity to my grandparents. I had made myself into the prissy young girl my new family and friends expected me to be – and I thought I would die of boredom. I was not really aware of how much I had changed until the new developments took place.

We had been staying put as much as possible, denying what was happening in the rest of the world. Mother continued with her soirees and *Kaffeeklatsches*, even after she became pregnant in the early fall of 1941. Such intimate details were discussed nightly at the dinner table, which it was my job to set up with beautiful Limoges china, Meissen on Sundays. Mother half regretted that I had to do such menial work but found solace in the thought that these tasks would make me into a very marriageable young woman. I found this laughable.

When I was 15 years old, in the early spring of 1944, Berlin was being bombed, and all children were commanded to evacuate, leaving parents to make impossible decisions. If one could prove that one had suitable private quarters somewhere in the countryside, one could be exempted. But gaining the exemption meant dealing with the likes of Herr Grotke, a formidable task for everyone with children. Nobody was told exactly where the children were to be sent, or when they would be able to see each other again.

I remember going to the provisional school in the morning

and passing groups of crying women. One, in the brown Hitler uniform, was telling everyone to keep their faces free of tears. The State would take care of everything. My school had been closed for some time to save fuel costs for the huge building that featured a four-story high rotunda, formerly adorned with bright brass railings. With the onslaught of war, the railings were confiscated to be made into shells and were replaced by wooden planks that by now were both unsightly and dangerous. The large fountain in the middle of the ground floor was covered with debris and had begun to smell musty. But, elite school that it was, such trifles did not deter us from our Tacitus or trigonometry. While the teaching staff consisted mainly of old men (who in their glory days had been professors and deans but were now deemed too old, too rebellious, or too Jewish to fight), the student body represented many old and influential families. While other families had to send their children off in dirty, shabby trains to unknown destinations, we spent our days in the huge dining room of a hotel that catered to the rich.

After Mother and I moved to Wilmerdorf, I was enrolled at The Cecilian Lyceum, a very different place from the *Dorotheen Oberschule* (Dorotheen High School) where I had begun my classical humanistic education. My new teachers did not try to hide their disdain for the "lower" order of girls and their working-class environment. I remember one woman in particular. She was said to be a well-known scholar but had a reputation for unfairly punishing pupils whom she didn't like. An early adherent of Hitler's party, she particularly disliked Jews and Communists. She openly remarked how sorry she was that her teaching schedule did not give her time to participate in the *Lebensborn* program, as she very much wanted to give a child to Hitler, "the greatest gift a woman can give to a man."

Another teacher, a Freiherrin (baroness) von und zu Lutzow, just as openly despised the *kleine Proleten mit grossen Alluren* (little working-class people with great pretensions) whom she had to teach. She had built a reputation as a scholar at a prestigious private school where she had run afoul of colleagues with different political orientations. She made no bones about this, telling the class how shameful she found it that "the sons of good families with good blood" were not impressed by her idol, Hitler.

I confessed I was bored in her classes, which always ended up with some paean to Hitler. I did the work with ease and then waited to see how she would twist National Socialism into her lectures. I was well-versed in the sophistry with which many adults justified their points of view and had acquired a reputation for being able to *herausreden,* to talk myself out of anything. When I talked Freiherrin von und zu Lutzow into a corner, she was furious and failed me for the semester.

Quite a few of my classmates were already looking for steady boyfriends. Like the Freiherrin, they yearned for babies, though not for the same reasons. It seemed that an unusual number of fathers felt entitled to fondle their daughters in secret, mainly when they were drunk. Having fortified themselves and made sure of their masculinity, they then donned their uniforms and followed in line behind Hitler, the Pied Piper of the Aryan Race. To judge by the tales their daughters told, incest was a way of life among some stalwarts who made just enough money or had just enough pull to obtain a *Freistelle* (scholarship) for their daughters.

I wasn't sure how much to believe of those open secrets, which were whispered with *Scheinheiligkeit* (hypocrisy), a great deal of revolting mimicry, handwringing, and even furious tears during our 15-minute breakfast break, which most of us spent standing in line to use the odiferous toilets. A best friend was always at hand to receive the tales and make sure others could hear them. One of the girls, Bettina, told on her father and then unwisely chose the Freiherrin as her confidante. Her father was compelled to withdraw her from school. We were told that it did not matter whether or not she had been abused. Even if it were true, Bettina would contaminate the rest of us, even me. When my turn arrived to lead the whispering, I tried to tell the girls that in the *Edda*, the collection of old Norse poems so beloved by the Nazis, Freya, the chief goddess, was forever complaining that her husband, the chief god Wotan, paid too much attention to the Valkyries, their presumed daughters.

When the time for evacuation drew near, the mysterious influential families got together and decided our fate. The Hotel Manager, Herr Zimpler, called us into his sumptuous office and informed us that our class had been chosen to be an example of "private evacuation" at its best. *Der Führer*, according to him, was interested in all of us, but would prefer if our families could provide for us, leaving more places for the Hitler Youth and other Nazi groups. We were to arrive at school the next morning at the usual time – 7:30 sharp if there had been no air raids the previous night or an hour later if bombs had interrupted our sleep. This had been the regular school schedule for some time.

I arrived home excitedly, thinking that Mother and I would have to do a bit of rushing around to meet our deadline. Much to my surprise, my suitcase was already packed with the allowable changes of underwear, a skirt, a sweater, a dress, and coats to be worn even in temperate weather. Mother had even sewn my name into each of my several pieces of clothing. To save even more space, the school instructed every second girl to leave her books at home.

I felt deflated. Here, I was finally part of a group that appeared to accept me and that held the promise of happy adventures. But even this feeling yielded to anxiety at the prospect of leaving. Walt's presence had lent my life a much-needed stability, and now he would be gone. After our move to Wilmersdorf, I experienced a new sense of being alone, without the protective wall of my family. I eventually became accustomed to using the cold bite of fear as both a signal of and defense against danger.

Mother sat me down in her most imperious way and motioned to me to do the same. "I hope we'll be able to bring you home in time for the baby's arrival," she said. "It won't be an easy birth at my age, but Walt needs an heir, and I want you to be directly under his nose during the whole process. He declined to adopt you so we have to make sure he thinks of you in a positive way."

And she continued: "We know where you are going, so we will be able to stay in touch. Your Uncle Wilhelm has his own seal by which we can mail letters anywhere." (Uncle Wilhelm was a brother of Oma Anna who had converted to Christianity and become a high-ranking civil servant in the German Post Office.) "Most importantly," she emphasized, "you must carry your American birth certificate everywhere, even when you sleep. Should you get in trouble, show it to whoever is misbehaving toward you and . . ." She faltered, and produced a little bag to be worn under my shirt. It irritated me immediately and I asked, "What will I do when we have to wash up?" She resumed her customary imperious posture, blew her nose, and informed me that she and Walt had decided to hide me "in plain sight, among the other girls." "Oh yes," she added, "Stay away from those Nazi kids. You know who I mean."

I knew, indeed. There were two or three girls in our group who boasted about their family's favored positions in the Party. They were not well-liked by the others, and I had joined in making sport of them, knowing they would eventually find a way to take revenge for my petty unkindnesses. Indeed, they already knew too much about me. When they tried to impress the rest of the class with their allegedly advance notice of our destination, I boasted in turn – and quite dramatically – about my Uncle Wilhelm and his seal. If they had bothered to pay attention, they might have deduced that being related to me, he might be Jewish as well and been on the road to a great triumph. I could already see the headlines: *Inspired Youths Expose Jew in High Post Office Position.* I vowed then and there to keep one step ahead of my enemies.

Our departure the next morning took place without a hitch. Parents had been told to stay away. Scenes at such partings were unwelcome. Responsible officials saw nothing exceptional in sending off groups of children to unknown destinations, particularly when they were all members of the *horere Klassen* (upper classes). After all, *Der Führer* had eliminated class consciousness. We met and drove for a while with a group of noisy boys our own age. Their bus was in worse condition than ours had been. The boys sang Nazi songs and tried in a rough way to make friends. They all claimed to be enrolled in a training course for entry into the Army, as officers of course. Gudrun and Freya, our two homegrown Nazi girls, did us proud by demonstrating beyond doubt that the boys were just showing off.

I was dealing with many feelings. First and foremost on my mind, when I was not preoccupied with school and chores, was my mother's pregnancy. I simply could not imagine my regal mother involved in the messy process of birth. As to what must have precipitated this situation . . . well, I really thought that the "upper classes" didn't do such things. I associated sex with the loud, noisy scenes on Erasmus Street and the earthy behavior of the women there. I had been given accurate information, but it did not penetrate my childish picture of human sexuality. That this information should somehow be connected to my mother's giving birth by someone other than my American father – this threw me into puzzlement and revived every negative word my paternal grandparents had ever uttered about my mother. And now I had to be hidden! Was I so much of a deviant? The old specter of Judaism raised its head again, and I resolved never to forget "from whence I came."

We finally arrived at a cloister where a dozen or so nuns had been praying for our safe arrival. There we resumed the kind of daily routine we had in Berlin. It seemed odd to do mathematics in the living room of a convent. We had large armchairs in which to recline, but they smelled of moth balls and dead flowers. The nuns now functioned as both teachers and governesses. They made us sit up straight and demerits were given for laxity; punishment took the form of being deprived of dessert. We stood in line to use the toilet and, with the nuns' zeal for cleanliness, our washed and rewashed hands soon reddened and resembled those of household servants. Much of our daily conversation concerned the war, about which we had little real knowledge. Food became scarce, and we all wrote letters home complaining about this unhappy fact of life.

One cold night, I climbed down from my top bunk in search of food and warmth. Instead of finding either, I bumped into one of my fellow prisoners who sat morosely, shivering in her nightgown. I chided her, "This is ridiculous, you can't sit here in your nightgown." She returned upstairs and I continued to wander the building alone. Suddenly, I heard a strange noise like the shattering of glass. My curiosity was piqued and I followed the sound, finding myself in the lower cellar. As my eyes adjusted to the gloom, to my surprise, a pair of trim legs covered by torn stockings appeared to be squeezing their way in through a broken window. To my amazement, my mother's full form – she was now five months pregnant – quickly followed. "Mother, be careful," I cried.

"Well, my pussycat. I find I've made it just in time."

"What do you mean?" I questioned.

She scoffed, "You are cut off from everything here! The Russians are advancing to the border, and you girls are in their path. Don't turn on the lights – they might see you from the shooting zone!"

We stood together momentarily and tried to figure out what to do. Mother said, "Wherever you can get in, you can also get out." She grabbed my hand and pulled me roughly out the window. I had no time to retrieve my belongings or a coat to protect me from the weather. Nearby the peasant who had been hired to return us to the station stood with a cart filled with straw and blankets. By the time we arrived, I was chilled and shivering. As we boarded the train, my mother was given a tattered coat while, for me, a hole was cut in a blanket that I wore like a poncho. The train sat stubbornly on the track with no indication of impending activity. As we sat, my mother informed me that she had learned that her unborn child was to be a boy. (She had scandalized her friends and family by consulting a village harridan who had performed an ancient rite involving a piece of string and a pebble.) I was upset with this news, even more than with my removal from what had become my new family. Now we would have to deal with a squalling baby on top of everything else! As the train made its way back toward home, it became clear that the province of Silesia had fallen to the Russians and refugees were trekking west by the thousands.

We returned to Berlin where life continued as usual. A new school was found in Potsdam, one with an illustrious history. I was to be part of an elite group living and studying at Sanssouci, the imposing summer palace of Frederick the Great, King of Prussia, built between 1745 and 1747 and with grounds modeled after Versailles. In recent years, it had been put into service as a place to educate the offspring of national heroes, transitioned briefly to a hospital facility, finally reverting back to a school. I was smitten with the place and delved into its history.

Many of my classmates were descendants of the most prominent families in the country, but my lack of a title left them no less interested in me. Some of the girls became good friends. One of them, Annette, was named after a famous poetess; this unfortunate girl had been raped and thrown into a canal, but, miraculously, she had recovered from this trauma and returned to school to pursue her education. We became quite close and, when the Russians were set to invade Berlin, I convinced my mother to take Annette with us. But she refused to leave her parents, and we set off for Anahoher without her. Despite her advanced pregnancy, Mother had managed to get a job in her Uncle Wilhelm's post office where, as it turned out, she garnered much useful information. It was through her post office contacts that she learned of the impending invasion of the Russian Army and began to plan our escape.

In the country at large, there was little enthusiasm for the many battles won by the German Army, especially the Siege of Leningrad that lasted 900 days. People were increasingly numb, either denying or ignoring the fact that the victories abroad were accompanied by a worsening situation at home. I had built my own armor that allowed me to cope fairly well with most any difficult situation. Like so many others, I focused inward and tried to distance myself from the unraveling world around me.

chapter eleven
A NEW PATH

The war ended quickly and without fanfare. It seemed that, instead of being happy that the danger was over, people had become depressed. I had never seen so many people who appeared to have escaped into their own interior worlds. Patriotism became a dirty word. The only activity that continued unabated was the consumption of beer. Housewives gave up washing their laundry, and the men stopped weaving their branches of willow.

I was preoccupied with my own dreams of relocation. My mother had her hands full with my stepfather, now quite depressed, and she was unavailable to me. He had managed to protect his small group of scientists from being taken over by the Red Army and, now in the hands of the Americans, he was still unable to design or manufacture any new products. The materials for such activities were simply not available, and so he complained to my mother daily: What had the fighting been about? What were we trying to achieve out of all of this?

While the two of them pondered our fate, I watched avidly while the American tanks and trucks rolled in. This was a thrilling event to me, although those around me were terribly afraid. The circle of scientists had shielded themselves from the truth that my stepfather had long been preaching to them: Hitler was a bum. Events led to an awakening, but the awakening was more like a living nightmare.

My mother also tried to keep us going as a family. She bartered lengths of thread for eggs and homemade beer for vegetables and fruit. One day she came home with news that the Russians were once again on the move and that Roosevelt had sold us down the river at Yalta. Her American friends had advised her to move west, and she was completely convinced this was the right thing to do. The Americans had made quite an impression when they rolled in with their huge tanks and numerous weapons. They also were very friendly to the populace and many of us, including my then three-year-old half-brother and me, received our first oranges. My brother had never seen an orange before. He had become, I confess, a charming child if ever there was one, with exceptional manners.

Mother was in a state of shock. She alternately muttered about her loss of illusions and her heroic but useless attempts to reestablish the Udebecks' social prominence. Somehow the length of time she had breastfed her son was held to play a role in this; after all, my annoying if adorable little brother "was also heir to social privileges." My mother shared her thoughts with a tall young man whom she befriended, as he had access to cigarettes and she to coffee, both highly prized commodities at the time. Her plan, with the threat of Russian occupation looming, was to send her children north where some relatives were eager to take us in. The tall, young tobacco man was enlisted as our caretaker for the trip. My stepfather fully supported this plan, offering "That's your mother's Slavic nature. They are more emotional than we northerners."

Mother dressed us warmly and made up a small suitcase for the two of us. She gave us a drink of nighttime tea and admonished me not to let my brother out of my sight. And off we went to the railroad station. We had been promised a first class compartment, but when the train rumbled in, there were only cattle cars. Our trusted "caretaker" threw us into one of them and then took off for parts unknown. I made a nest for us near the stove where we might get some sleep.

My brother lay down and was immediately asleep, but I was not to be so lucky. As soon as I lay down, a hand began to crawl up my body, and it dawned on me that a man was trying to have sex with me. I moved away but he followed and tried again. I told him "NO" loudly enough to draw the attention but not the assistance of the women in the compartment. Someone advised me to lie back and enjoy it. Terrified and convinced my brother would awaken and fall out of the train, I tied him to my belt. He endured the trip without knowledge of the attempted rape.

A day later, we arrived in Hamburg, where there was a sprawling camp for displaced persons, wounded individuals from both sides of the war, and persons with other official designations. As usual, I did not fit into any of the categories. Fortunately, a nice lady from the Red Cross took us under her wing. She brought us to her tent, gave us donuts and sweetened coffee, and put us to bed on her warm cot. After filling out many forms and being shuffled back and forth, I was told I could depart right then and there for America. But what would come of my brother, who was 100 percent German? I couldn't leave him alone in such a place, so we stayed at the camp and lived day to day until, about a month later, my mother appeared to collect us. True to form, she almost strangled our new friend, the Red Cross lady, and hauled us off in her private car, driven by the ever-present Schloske.

In the months following the war, the question of where one could live was paramount. We were fortunate to acquire a truly magnificent address. For once Mother was satisfied. We lived at Castle Adelstein in a remote region of Germany that was neither pretty nor prestigious, but had at least been spared much suffering during the war. An intensely patriotic folk lived there who viewed Hitler as one of those unavoidable natural catastrophes, like the great famine of 1780 or the use of mustard gas in the First World War.

The villagers were forgiving. When the damaged men arrived and abused their wives, they sagely nodded saying: "What can you expect?" After all, these sons of Germany were patriots, so all was understandable from their point of view. "The Fatherland above all" was their motto. Nobody asked their wives and children how they felt about being beaten by patriots.

Patriots or not, the farmers of the region went about their planting and seeding and weeding and harvesting as they always had. In a show of the old, genuine patriotism that had nothing to do with Hitler, their wives upheld the customs of times gone by. For instance, they wore the local costume on Sundays and didn't seem the least bit worried about being totally out of style. What had been good enough for their great-great-grandmothers was good enough for them. When they danced their staid dances in the village square, accompanied by a badly tuned brass band, their heavy embroidered skirts flew half way up their square bodies and revealed lace trimmed pantaloons with slits and buttons in strategic places. Tightly corseted by whale bone reinforced waistcoats fastened with genuine gold or silver coins, they could hardly breathe. Their faces would turn red while their breath imitated the coal-fed railroad which, even now, so soon after the destruction of most of the German infrastructure, puffed its steam-driven way through the hills and dales of a part of the country that appeared totally disinterested in the bloody drama to which it had been unwitting host.

The men, somewhat more cognizant of the fate of the land

they truly loved, rhythmically hoisted their nail-studded shoes and slapped their thighs in somewhat embarrassed imitation of ancestral glee. They were mostly very old men whose tales had more to do with the First World War than the Second one. But they knew the ritual dances in their bent bones and fiercely beating hearts. They'd be damned if they would let the rich foreign conquerors see them as anything but strong enough to bring in the harvest. When occupying forces marched by, they started spitting in the conquerors' direction, slyly masking their contempt with recourse to old mens' need to cough.

The youngsters, who had never known anything but the Thousand Year Empire, vacillated between their Hitler youth gear and the leather shorts and corduroy shirts of the regional costumes. Their dancing was clumsy and arrhythmic, and they could hardly lift their hefty dance partners. Their reluctant mien conveyed loudly that the women were too old and less than satisfactory partners. They much preferred spending their time at the gate to the encampment of the occupying forces, where they could shout: "Hey, G. I. Joe, you got gum?" They all sought to make friends with soldiers and to get their leftover rations and cigarette butts.

How did we find our way to this elegant, if now threadbare, address? We came to the castle through the US army, which sought Walt's expertise. The Americans gathered up whomever they could among the scientists that fell into their hands, among them the research and development group to which Walt, with several inventions to his name, belonged. But rather than making themselves dependent on the Americans, scientists in Walt's group asked for, and were granted permission to establish, their own quarters. Where to put a bunch of highly individualistic, absent-minded professor-types and their more or less "upper class" families, most – but not all – of whom had opposed Hitler? Castle Adelstein, in this forgotten corner of Germany, seemed as good a solution as any.

Elated by the apparent privilege of living without MPs

watching us, we moved into the damp castle with its fifteenth-century thick walls, huge rooms, and inadequate plumbing. The rooms were very large, so there was no way each family could have a domicile of its own. Instead, we were divided into the "young maidens," "the bachelors," "the newlyweds," and the "leading families." Each group was given one of the ballroom-size rooms, some wooden planks, nails and hammers and instructed to do what they could to make themselves comfortable. We were enjoined to be grateful for the material and tools, which were rare in those postwar years. When we woke up in the refrigerator-like temperature of our first morning in the castle (on mattresses on the floor), we discovered that half our supplies had disappeared.

Trained by Walt to problem-solve, I had already made friends with two other "young maidens." Together we stacked what wood we could get hold of in a corner, gathered up strewn nails, and stashed them in empty spaces behind wooden panels that hid the venerable walls of our new home. We later learned that the wainscoting had been installed quite recently, in 1850 or so, while the castle itself had been built around the time of the last crusades, in the fifteenth century. Indoor plumbing did not exist but right next to the entrance to the former castle keep were four outhouses, two each for men and women. There were about 30 of us all told.

While Lieselotte, Hannelore, and I organized our supplies, my mother fainted, my brother screamed, Lieselotte's mother threatened divorce, and Hannelore's mother cried. The two newlywed couples were as busy as my friends and me, erecting small barriers around mattresses and declaring the partitioned space their "homes."

The newlyweds disappeared behind their make-shift walls, and we "young maidens" were sorely tempted to peek through the many spaces left between the boards. But Lieselotte shrugged her shoulders. "Those guys aren't worth it," she informed us. "They didn't take them into the army, so they're probably impotent. Mother said they took every man with a drop of German blood in them. My mother was the head of the North German Coalition of Mothers, so she knew what went on. We needed more babies to fight for us but most women only wanted a husband and many children." "So bourgeois," she sniffed. Hannelore laughed: "That's what they are all supposed to be, either bourgeois or proletarian. My mother said that refined people like us don't stand a chance."

I didn't think I would stand a chance with such refined people, Nazi or not. I wished my mother would stop fainting and stop spoiling my brother, who was nearly school-age. It was downright embarrassing to be reminded three or four times a day that Mother had chosen to become a housewife. I wouldn't have been surprised if she had made friends with Lieselotte's mother and become one of the heroines of the Nazi women's coalition; the title "Heroine of Motherhood" got you a medal and 100 RM per month when you had four kids. I wondered how all this would change, now that the Americans were here. So far, they seemed to have brought us military government, anti-fraternization laws, and a lot of displaced persons who were angry at the preferential treatment our small group was being given. I also wondered how Lieselotte's mother would react if she found out she was living in the same house as Jews.

An interesting young man had appeared in our rather shabby digs. He claimed to have walked all the way from North Germany to our encampment. His motivation had been, supposedly, me. He had seen me at the event that had "launched 1000 ships." I couldn't remember Uwe at all. Nor was I impressed by his father, the General, as he was known, who had apparently changed his loyalties from his Jewish wife to his half-Jewish son. Of course, I knew how it felt to be a mongrel and was not nearly as nasty to Uwe as I could have been.

The young man soon became an item in our bachelors'

quarters. I was convinced that he only wanted a safe place to hide, though I also knew he desperately wanted a girlfriend as a badge of advancement among all these scientists and engineers. I was interested in boys and decided to give him a chance, but one whiff of his *Lederhosen* and the inside of his military coat nipped any budding attraction. He eventually fell in love with my sophisticated friend, Hannelore, whom he later married. But that is her story. My epiphany at the time was that a man could smell so vile that it was impossible to fall in love with him.

If I thought of boys at all, I thought of the fellow who had scrunched a note into my hand on our original flight from Berlin. He had absolutely beautiful blue eyes, and he was obviously looking to make contact. He wore his torn, many-times mended officer candidate uniform with grace, and, as it turned out, he was also a fabulous dancer. We met in my best girlfriend's apartment, where we danced away, sharing only minimal details about our lives. For me, it was the first budding of sexual attraction. We both promised to stay in touch, knowing full well this would be well-nigh impossible because of the war.

As we settled in to our new environment, Mother was careful to avoid sensitive subjects like a visit to my grandmother or the possibility of my emigrating to America. As to the latter notion, she held back nothing. "You are NOT going to America. I forbid it. We've come through the war better than most. The family is together. So what are you plotting against your own mother?"

I had learned long ago that the best thing to do when Mother was overwrought was to say nothing. She would either escalate her tirades or faint. The fainting used to frighten me, since she looked like a dead person after falling on the floor. I used to run and fetch cold compresses and some sherry to pour into her mouth. She'd sputter and cough and "come to herself" with all the drama of a Victorian aristocrat. She had me fooled until one day I noticed that she had a trick of looking at the scene before her under skillfully lowered eyelids. She didn't miss a thing. The length and depth of her "spells" depended on the number of people present and how many she needed to control. When I shared my thoughts on this matter with Walt, he became furious and forbade me ever to talk like that again. His wife was merely over sensitive and deep. And then for emphasis: They were planning to send me to a school where respect for parents was instilled, not the free and easy type of *internat* (boarding school) to which I had become accustomed.

My thoughts of America had struck a sensitive nerve in my mother. I actually had the audacity to want to leave her and Germany. And it was true: I couldn't wait to get out of there. After all the years of being an outsider, of being unwanted because I was an American by birth and a Jew, I looked forward to going home to MY America. I envisioned a country where all my fantasies would come true, even those I knew could not. I wanted to be a femme fatale, a famous and celebrated ballerina who had men at her feet, but also a healer like my Oma Anna. I also wanted to try out "necking," a sort of love-making not in favor among "our set." Listening to my mother with only half my attention, I heard one of her preposterous pronouncements: "After all we've been through you want to leave, just at the point when the cancer in the breast of our beloved country has been removed, and we can build a society based on merit and social standing."

I made a mistake and muttered: "Maybe your country, not mine." This sort of retort regularly infuriated her even further. She began to stutter, her words tumbling over each other inchoately. As long as she kept talking I knew there was no danger of one of her spells grounding her. As I composed myself to endure more tales about the refinement of the German upper crust in the past, I simultaneously saw her sweeping the ashes of the millions of her own under the expensive oriental rug she was proud to have "liberated" from our old apartment in Berlin.

An entirely different agenda had begun to take shape in my mind. I was going to travel to America and find my biological father. The fact that I had no money and no passport did not deter me. I was sure something would come up to facilitate my plans. Didn't it always? Hadn't I traveled by myself in cattle cars and stinking compartments through air raids and territory riddled by fighting? I felt mature and ready to take on the world. And Mother, in the period prior to my departure, would be able to use my new American passport to bring all sorts of belongings over the border drawn by the allies in their effort to castrate Germany forever. Indeed, having an American passport in the family would be the ticket to all kinds of wonderful privileges. This was the reason she had relented and let me get the passport at all.

But obtaining my passport proved a great adventure and deserves a chapter of its own.

chapter twelve
A PASSPORT

To get my American passport I would have to travel to Munich, where the temporary American consulate was located. How could I do this? Neither the telephone nor the telegraph worked, so it was impossible to ascertain train schedules. Travelers simply got on the train they thought went in their general direction and hoped for the best. Mother quickly forbade me from becoming one of these railroad gypsies; she was sure I would be raped if I joined "those vagabonds" in an effort to reach Munich.

But I wanted my passport and began a campaign to convince Walt I could be trusted to undertake the journey to the consulate. I had a fantasy of a consul as a handsome man in a Roman toga and laurel leaf headband handing out parchment scrolls that established American citizenship beyond any doubt. With such a document in hand, how could I fail to make it to the United States?

It took Walt's secretary and me three days to reach Munich in a contraption that had once been a large Diesel-powered

Mercedes. Of course it was out of the question to buy fuel of any kind legally. We were lucky that mother had managed to parley the promise of my fully documented American citizenship into permission to travel at all. She further apprised us of the danger of falling into the hands of illiterate and coarse Russian soldiers who would not be able to read our papers. Why she thought we would encounter Russians in American territory was lost on me, but then who knew where Mother's flights of fancy came from or where they might lead her.

After Mother obtained our travel permits, she commissioned Schloske, our driver, to buy a lot of kindling and wood. The back seat of his Mercedes limousine was removed to make room for the wood which, as it burned, produced a kind of gas that was piped into what looked like a hot water heater mounted on the open trunk of the car. Being the youngest, I had to sit on the wood. We stayed overnight at inns which had until recently housed refugees, displaced persons, and soldiers. One inn, which had been a command post for some German officers, was relatively intact, but in the others, we had to make do with beds that had no sheets and with toilets that looked as though they had not been flushed in months.

We had to bring our own provisions, supplemented by the purchase in one place of cabbage-and-potato soup; the owner remembered Walt's staying there in "better times." Of course I was warned to keep my mouth shut because one still could not be sure who was loyal to the Nazis and who had welcomed the liberators. It was obvious to me that everyone we met would have preferred the "old order." It just wasn't always clear whether the old order was the Nazis or the aged Kaiser Wilhelm, who was said to reside in The Hague.

Our trip was not so easy. I kept getting splinters in my thighs, my dress, once my Sunday best, having long been outgrown. The splinters in my thighs started to fester almost immediately, and I felt conspicuous in the short dress. So I was glad when we ran out of wood even though it meant we could not go much farther. Schloske saved the day. He found a traveling salesman who was stranded but had a father-in-law in a nearby village who owned a piece of woodland. We agreed to give him a ride, even though this was against the law. In exchange, we would receive a stock of wood that would take us all the way to Munich. For an unguarded instant, I wished Mother were there. She would have driven a much harder bargain.

The salesman proved to be a lascivious turd. Sitting with me in the back on top of the remaining wood, he noticed me surreptitiously trying to extricate some splinters and remove, with saliva, the sap of the wood from my legs. Chattering cheerfully he inserted his hand between my legs. When I batted him away, he grabbed at my breast, and I screamed. But Schloske couldn't pull over because just then an American army convoy swooped down the narrow road. Nor could we use the highway, Hitler's famed *Autobahn*, because of the dangers presented by army units who wouldn't recognize our travel papers, discharged German soldiers, and plain old-fashioned highwaymen. Walt made some ineffectual gesture toward the back while the salesman continued to enjoy himself hugely. He grabbed my other breast and wrestled me on my back, "Don't worry, Father," he said. "The little twit enjoys it."

He didn't know who he was dealing with. I grabbed one of the pieces of wood and swung at him at the same time as Schloske managed to drive off the road in an effort to dislodge the man. We all rolled to one side in a muddy field. The car sputtered to a halt. "You won't get far," the salesman threatened. "They know me for many kilometers around here. Do you think anyone would believe you for one minute?" The car was on a slant, making it impossible to open the doors on that side. Schloske and the man exploded out the front doors at the same time, with Walt huffing after them. Schloske, a former wrestling champion, soon had him in a headlock while Walt tried to wrest the piece of wood out of my hand, as I continued to beat the hapless guy. As it turned out, we still needed him, as the wood we had bought was so wet it didn't make a sufficient amount of vaporous gas.

Walt then did something that I hated and that usually didn't work. But in this situation, it was exactly what was called for. He pulled himself up to his full height, braced his back with one arm, and pronounced each ringing syllable: "Do you know who I am, my man? You should be careful whom you assault." And then he ticked off a list of people that he was related to. Most of the time when it came to that, nobody knew what he was talking about. He put such unresponsiveness down to the social chaos created by the Nazis, and readily forgave such lapses of good manners. He felt one couldn't expect too much from such benighted people. But in this unlikely situation, on a muddy field in Bavaria, it did the trick. The salesman was someone who yearned for the "old order" and protested that he had merely adapted to the Nazis. He took us to "a customer" of his who had "connections." Two burly Bavarians in filthy *Lederhosen* (leather shorts) were summoned and commanded to saw a huge oak the customer had stored in his barn. At the same time, a group of villagers pulled the limo out of the mud. They seemed to have a good time. When we were finally on our way again, Schloske asked Walt to drive.

"Those were bandits, sir. It's a wonder they let us off with our lives and the Fräulein with her honor intact." Then he stuck his head out of the window and vomited. Walt drove the rest of the way to Munich.

The villages we passed looked just as they always had; some well taken care of and prosperous even in those desperate times, some run down and barely inhabitable. The aftermath of yet another war lost and another generation perverted by false pride, secret rage, and stubborn belief in the magic of discipline was almost palpable. In my household, these values were admired but not emulated. Mother and Walt thought of themselves as part of an elite that behaved in a dignified and "correct" manner as a matter of course. I was supposed to absorb this sense of correctness through osmosis, but it turned out that my grandparents' value system had undermined the standards Walt was born to and that Mother adopted as her own.

As we drove on, I was so buoyed by the thought of receiving my very own passport, my ticket to an America where I would be safe forever, that I hardly noticed that we were driving through streets lined with rubble and occasionally large piles of bricks, cleanly stacked up upon one other and counted. Large white numerals gave an eerie effect, like murals begun in leisure and then abandoned in haste. There was also a pervasive odor that I could not place.

As we entered Munich, we came to a street crossing that looked like a giant child's sand castle game, with broad, straight avenues running in all directions. An American soldier was directing scant traffic, mainly army vehicles of all kinds. Walt gasped, "They bombed everything. There are no houses . . ." I woke out of my pleasant reverie. "You've seen other places like that. You said it was necessary to clean the cancer on the breast of Germany," I said by way of consolation. We had seen bombing; we'd had bombs rain down upon us; we lived through burial in an air raid shelter. So what was all the fuss?

"Callow brat," he blurted out. "There was the little palais here where royal rulers lived in my youth . . ." he choked up again. "But you said . . ." But before I could go on, he gasped again. "Sacrilege! They put their miserable headquarters in the Royal Orangerie [green house]. I suppose the heating was still intact there. Look, there are some of the exotic plants the prince liked, still intact."

I had never seen him so emotional before. But before I could voice surprise, he turned on me again: "And don't talk such nonsense in my presence again." Ordinarily, I would have reminded him that I was merely repeating his wife's, my mother's, words. But not this time. He had directed such emotion toward me only once before, when I introduced him to my new American friends as my stepfather. As usual in our household, telling the truth brought dire consequences. Walt couldn't understand how irksome it was to have an entirely German family, and how eager I was to meet my American father who was, after all, my biological father.

"I didn't deserve that from you," he said. And I suppose he was right. He had sent me from one member of his large family to another, from anti-Hitler cousins and old aunts to longtime family retainers. He had paid my high school and boarding school tuitions and then paid for my tutors when private schools were closed by the government. He had provided safe haven for me and probably saved my life more than once.

Schloske was acutely uncomfortable. He didn't like scenes either. And I suppose that he had endured more than enough embarrassment witnessing Mother's fainting spells, on occasion having to revive her when no one else was around. I am sure he was devastated by Walt's hysterical outburst. It did not match his view of how a Prussian gentleman should behave.

The smell I had noticed before became even stronger. Dad wrinkled his nose. "What the deuce is this? I suppose those Americans put their consulate in the Orangerie as well. They would, wouldn't they? Pull up to that preposterous policeman and ask him where to go." Schloske complied. "There aren't any other buildings standing, sir," he said in his well-trained servant manner. We pulled up to the policeman, who was as puzzled as we were. He saluted briskly and walked around us, inspecting the weird vehicle in which we sat. We noticed that he wore a dirty surgical mask.

"Are you all right buddy?" Schloske became chummy, noting the man's interest in the car. "She's a beauty, she is, the wave of the future, mark my word. We can't always depend on oil and you Americans to supply it. But what smells here, Bud?"

The American understood a little German. "It's the dead bodies they couldn't get to yet. It'll take a while before everyone is found and buried properly," he informed us.

I felt numb, completely numb, and had to ask myself if I had really heard what the MP had said. Somehow my inner world had become attuned to a black-and-white outer world. Either I dealt with bad Germans who were intent on killing me or good Americans who wanted to save me. I could allow for certain exceptions, like the people, mainly members of my stepfather's extended clan, who had helped me stay alive. But I had already figured out that they abhorred Hitler for all the wrong reasons. My mother cried when she heard that Goebbels had killed himself and his family, and she was even more distressed when Göring did away with himself. According to her, he had belonged to the Old Guard of honorable gentlemen who were seduced by Hitler's false promises of reclaiming their one-time dominance.

But here, in this old city that I connected with jolly beer drinkers and free sex, I had to face the fact that I would literally have to ride over and around relatively fresh corpses before I could get my American passport. At that moment, it didn't matter to me that the corpses were German. Grief hit me like a thunderbolt. Death appeared in a new form: Dead is dead and is terrible for the people who are not ready for it. Strangely, it dawned on me that I myself had managed to be ready for death. Years later, I understood how this readiness helped me to be fearless during situations that are not exactly part of a normal childhood. For the time being, I fantasized about My America, where I would receive everything I had missed, though I could not then imagine what exactly I had missed.

The MP waved us on. Schloske looked close to vomiting. Dad took over the wheel while I momentarily thought myself in a fearful land of vampires. We did not then know the details about the concentration camps, but we had heard terrible rumors that only Walt believed. My mother, faux noblewoman that she was, simply refused to believe that the horror really occurred.

Eventually we arrived at a gate house and were waved into what I thought were formal English Gardens. We parked and were guided to a rundown building. The double doors swung open to a pandemonium of desperation: The sour smell of unwashed bodies, foul clothing, poorly disinfected wounds, mouth odor, rotting vegetables, and kerosene replaced the stink of death outside. The three of us stood in silence. Schloske whimpered: "And we thought we had it tough."

The people around us looked as though they couldn't take another step, even though everyone had made an attempt to look decent. One could see the effort that had gone into patching together ill-fitting garments, and their rags were brushed. Some women, relatively young, wore lipstick on prematurely toothless mouths. A couple of young children clung fiercely to their caretakers, and a few teenagers lounged about in what they took to be the nonchalant American style. Everyone smoked; American cigarettes were readily available in the black market but were very expensive. In all, this crew of people looked as though they could not afford 5RM for the thin artificial coffee one could order in some of the newly opened cafés. Amid the confusion, Walt took charge. Smiling politely, he explained: "My daughter is an American citizen. Surely the consul will want to see her first." The man grinned: "So I also. *Nix versteli.*"

A woman strode over to us in queenly fashion. She puffed away under a great straw hat, the brim of which was so close to her cigarette that I was afraid it would catch fire. With her ivory cigarette holder, yellow with use, the woman looked elegant but used. Dad gallantly kissed her hand, a habit he had abandoned some time ago, explaining that it no longer suited the times. In truth the times no longer suited him. Like my mother, he yearned for the well-ordered, benign feudal system of his youth. My mother of course had never experienced that sort of life, though she constantly reminded all and sundry what splendid privileges she had enjoyed before the war. The two mourned their fantasies together.

But this was the American consulate, as shabby as the rest of Germany and occupied by a shabby crowd of would-be Americans. The tarnished grand lady graciously offered Dad a cigarette. "One cannot live without them. One needs them like an anesthetic," she remarked. "Everyone here claims to be an American. Some of these people seem to think that the Americans have the same laws as the Great Thousand Year Empire of that janitor Hitler. They think they are like the *Reichsdeutschen* from the Volga or the Ukraine. You have only to be a fourth- or fifth-generation German to be assured room in tiny Germany. So these idiots assume that if they have an aunt in Brooklyn or an uncle in Chicago they are American citizens as well."

Schloske, despite his generally discreet behavior, smirked and left to guard the car. Walt watched him leave and sighed: "Employees are not what they used to be." "I know, I know," the woman commiserated. "One's *staff* does not know how to act anymore."

They both avoided the word they really meant. Most Germans did not know how Americans behaved toward *servants,* or even whether, in a democracy, it was appropriate to think of persons employed domestically as servants. I hardly recognized Walt in his smooth, gentle approach to this female stranger. Perhaps, I thought, Mother was not faithful and Dad was the injured party. Could it be that she had learned that sort of behavior from him along with his cultured fantasies of past familial glory? As the two were still ogling each other, one of the well-pressed, clean-cut Americans opened an inside door and was nearly squashed to death against the wall when the throng threw itself toward him, each person waving some piece of paper to substantiate his or her claims.

The American seemed used to this. Walt blew a kiss to our new acquaintance, who ostentatiously ignored the gesture. When the general excitement abated somewhat, the man began to call out some names. "Nothing for you today, Frau Baronin," he finished.

Dad pushed me forward. "Here, this is my daughter. You must have her name? We are here to obtain her American passport."

"This girl is your daughter? How is that? The money for her passage has already been guaranteed by her father. So how are you her father, buddy?"

Frau Baronin was suddenly beside herself: "You can actually leave! You have an American citizen in the family. She will vouch for you and then your family can go to America."

The flirtation was suddenly over. Dad bowed formally: "Delighted to have met you, Frau Baronin. But what would happen to Germany if all of us leave?" He pushed me further toward the man who waived me into his office. A few questions later, he stamped the little green book that held the key to my future. I would go to America and meet my real father.

13.
chapter thirteen
OCCUPATION

Getting around in those postwar years was very difficult. Trains and buses seemed to have a mind of their own, arriving and departing at whimsical times, like 4:00 a.m. Sometimes they stopped at this or that station, other times they did not. Sometimes there were only first-class carriages strung together. People hesitated to get on because they did not know how much extra they would have to pay despite the threadbare conditions of the compartments. At other times there were only cattle cars, their doors wide open, displaying rotting straw and an occasional potbelly stove. All trains reeked of urine and human sweat, sometimes of excrement. Those intent on figuring out the schedules of these hapless conveyances were bound to end up doubting their sanity.

Given these uncertainties, families camped out on the railroad platforms permanently, officiously monopolizing the water faucets and toilets. Some travelers made it their business to stand guard at the facilities and collect small fees for letting others use them. In the meantime, these denizens of a new kind of gypsy life spun tales that made them appear creators of a new lore of the rails. They told of trains that were impervious to stations. Their favorite ruse was to stop in the middle of nowhere as well as in ruined stretches of rubble left from air attacks or combat. And even though the war had officially ended, there were still some fanatics with machine guns and rifles who killed people because, it was said, "they had not kept the faith with *Führer und Vaterland.*

Everyone looked to the occupying forces to bring order, and they did so very efficiently. Each settlement, village, town, and city had a military governor, usually the ranking officer of the unit that had conquered the area. These men were given orders that they passed on to the anxious populace. There was to be no fraternization, a curfew was strictly enforced, and travel from place to place was forbidden. Only those privileged few whose work brought them into contact with the Americans could sometimes obtain a travel permit. And then, all the permit did was make it legal to use the derelict trains. Quickly, a black market in real and forged travel documents sprang up like weeds on rubble.

The non-fraternization law was a sham as well. GIs careening along in their well- fueled jeeps merrily waved at girls and young women, wolf-whistled, and held out Hershey bars and gum as enticements to take a ride. They weren't aware that their passengers would have climbed aboard without much encouragement, as many of them had never traveled in a car before. The thought of going in such style from town to town was so alluring to the young female population that many of the GIs used their jeeps as a way to get girlfriends. Nobody stopped them, and the older folk soon began to grumble about the lack of discipline in the US forces. They would never have gotten away with such disobedience in the German Army, no way. Why a guy could get shot for such behavior!

Mother busied herself bartering for food while telling any American who would listen about her daughter, who was a

Elaine at 17, during the American occupation, serving as interpreter for American GIs and the German girl to her left

bonafide US citizen. She had given up fainting and assumed the role of master purchasing agent. If her own mother had been with her, Oma would have been exchanged for groceries or a ham. Mother sometimes dragged me out to meet some embarrassed officer – nobody under the title of second lieutenant was socially acceptable for barter with Mother – in order to substantiate her claims for whatever cigarettes, candy, or food were available from the PX. She kept us well fed and enlightened the occupiers about any mistake they made. For instance, she alerted them to the fact that quite a few of the farmers sold whatever foodstuffs they had rather than feeding their children. Therefore, Mother thought, the evacuees' children should get as much or more of the food the American Red Cross soup kitchens were doling out. She managed to charm the local military governor into allowing me to shop in the PX, something that was strictly prohibited.

She also perfected a spellbinding account of our past and future. Deepening her voice to a Marlene Dietrich growl, she would shudder expressively and tell of her days hidden in "vile cottages on Bavaria's mountain tops, only a few kilometers removed from the life-giving borders of Switzerland." Oh, how she had yearned for freedom, and how she regretted having miscalculated the influence upon the populace of that despicable criminal Hitler, who did not even know which fork to use when! No, it was too, too dreadful, this internal attack upon the spiritual Germany that, once upon a time, had showered largesse on people like her. And perhaps the Major, or Captain, or Colonel had some nylons in his luggage, or some real coffee?

Mother suffered from lack of coffee and cigarettes. When she did her "regrets oratorio," as I came to think of her tirades, she neglected to add that she was born in Poland and that the "vile cottage" was the vacation home of a Jewish refugee who Mother, when a bank employee, had helped send money out of the country. She held firm to her "elitist principles" and bartered only with officers, even after she discovered that sergeants of all kinds probably had greater access to goods than their superiors.

The U.S. army, like the German one, was fond of keeping their soldiers sharp and combat ready. Combat readiness included sending patriots out to inspect everyone's identification papers. On occasion they visited Adelstein as well. Some wound up in the charming decayed pub, drinking homemade beer and wine with English-speaking patrons. All the while Mother was enticing young officers to find her whatever was needed in our new household. Makeshift though our quarters were, Mother and Walt exerted themselves to maintain appearances: Their shoes were always polished to a high shine, Walt always wore his single remaining tie, and Mother darned everyone's socks while trying to look both glamorous and domestic.

Well, she didn't quite darn everyone's socks. Mine were excluded. At 16, I was supposed to follow in her footsteps. She was embarrassed that I was plainly aware of the shift in the power base of our small family, and angry that I would not consent to her schemes.

This was the time when I had two boyfriends. One was a handsome German with improbably blue eyes who had been an officer candidate in some elite war college. Just three years older than I, he kissed hands and clicked heels divinely. He also danced well. My friends Lieselotte and Hannelore swooned when he arrived at Castle Adelstein in search of his father. He owned nothing at all, not even clothes, and wore his army uniform inside out in order not to be taken for a deserter. His father, a well-known scientist, was known by some of Walt's colleagues. The ladies were also smitten with him. They pleaded with Walt to let him stay in the cavernous bachelor's quarters and raided their husbands' scant supply of clothing to supply Uwe with a minimum of civilian comfort. It took all of my mother's ingenuity to parlay her U.S. contacts into an order for the Mayor of Adelstein to issue a new ID and food coupons for him.

I was simultaneously enchanted with Luke, an American lieutenant with black hair much too long for a soldier. He wore drooping fatigues and a revolver, elegantly low and useless, hanging from a civilian belt somewhere in the vicinity of his slim hips. He had been drinking homemade beer and wine with Lieselotte's mother when I came to pick up my friend for one of the many walks during which we read poetry to one another and assumed what we thought to be appropriately melancholy demeanors.

As it turned out, Luke thought me "striking" and instead of seducing Lieselotte's mother or bartering with mine, returned the next afternoon with flowers for me and coffee for my mother. I was speechless. Nothing like that had ever happened to me before and, in some odd way, I was indignant. How dare he court me when Lieselotte's mother clearly wanted him? Lieselotte was aware of this too, and beseeched me not to succumb to him. "Mother will be impossible to live with if she doesn't get him," she told me breathlessly. "You know she used to go to the *Lebensborn* to be an example to other German women and to make more Aryan babies. She never got pregnant there, though."

I didn't think Walt would go for Mother attending a *Lebensborn*. He thought the whole idea an abomination, even though it stilled some women's sexual hunger. I was eager to experience sexual hunger too, but so far I felt only mildly titillated when Uwe clicked his heels and kissed my hand. My inner energy was focused upon imaginings about America. Luke interested me because he could tell me more about that fabulously free land where teenagers did something called "necking" without anybody interfering. I thought the emphasis on the neck was odd and hypothesized that I probably was not cut out to be a great tragedienne with several lovers in distress if this involved only the neck.

Lieselotte thought I was too healthy looking for a great dramatic life, although she agreed with Hitler for once that a healthy sex life made for better health. Neither of us had the slightest idea what constituted a healthy sex life, but we knew that we didn't have it. Uwe seemed reluctant to go further than to kiss my hand and signaled to me that he had chosen me by not kissing Lieselotte's hand any more. She didn't mind because she thought she was in love with a husky farmer's son who had a lot of bushy hair and habitually wore the traditional farmer's smock.

The farmer's son had been in the German army and was said to be experienced. Uwe looked like a splendid scarecrow next to this village swain. He had clothes now but, because it was not possible to buy anything except on the black market, he had to make do with odds and ends given him by the ladies in our group. He often wore a white poet's shirt with huge sleeves. It had belonged to Lieselotte's mother. With the addition of a ragged black cravat from Walt, previously worn to funerals or when he had to meet the military governor, it gave the appearance of a man's garment. Uwe's lower extremities were less elegantly covered in his shabby *Lederhosen*, the leather shorts favored by Bavarian and other peasants.

Hannelore and Lieselotte's mother, however, did not take Uwe's desertion so kindly. Lieselotte swore that her mother had a crush on Uwe, calling him the personification of "glowing, everlasting youth," of which she apparently hoped to partake. Hannelore thought both of us were wrong and that she herself was really Uwe's favorite; he just hadn't gotten around to speaking to her yet, preoccupied as he was with warding off Lieselotte's mother and me. She followed me around when I was alone and all but spat on me. No one had ever stalked me before, and I didn't know what to do. There I was, having done absolutely nothing, in the middle of an unfolding drama in which I took Luke away from a woman my mother's age – strange that she was interested in the same thing I was! – and was simultaneously courted by a gorgeous German. I should have been thrilled but I wasn't. I wanted to go to America. America was my true love.

Luke was not put off by my plans. He began to recite poetry to me, mainly by someone named Walt Whitman, who was inordinately fond of leaves and grass. Luke also composed some lyrical verses about and for me, and tried to look deep into my eyes while I squirmed and tried to wriggle out of his manly arms. Uwe also discovered a poetic streak and began composing a long poem about finding love while reading to me Goethe's *Hermann und Dorothea* – when, that is, neither my brother nor the mosquitoes were bothering us.

I rather enjoyed all this, but my mother made sure that there was little unsupervised time. I became more and more uneasy about all the attention and about losing Hannelore's respect.

She told all and sundry that I was hanging out with Americans in order to receive gifts. With mounting internal pressure, I determined silently that the time had come. I had to go to America, where I belonged.

In the meantime, Mother made my recently acquired passport work for her in her black market dealings. And Walt was only too content to keep his mouth buttoned as she went about her dealings. In the helter-skelter of the postwar period, he realized it was wise to let Mother assume the role of breadwinner, black market wheeling-dealing and all. And in truth there was some justification for her behavior. The local baker, butcher, and grocer sold their scant goods only to the locals. They all expressed their contempt for city-bred evacuees by ignoring us with much pomp and circumstance. For instance, Herr Schinkel, the butcher, would cut and weigh a piece of meat, wrap it ceremoniously into a piece of newspaper, hand it over to a farmer's wife as though it was the crown jewels of England, and then smirk at whichever woman in our group had come to him for the weekly ration of meat and humiliation.

Herr Schinkel seemed to have gotten us mixed up with the Nazis who, in his empty mind, were members of the "new ruling class." I surmised that he had not yet noticed the war was over. Somehow, our meat ration was always tough and bony or fatty. My mother cut off the fat and reduced it with apples and onions, making it into a delicious spread for the coarse bread Herr Kohle, the baker, was occasionally good enough to sell us.

The other women were aghast and the men envious at my mother's expertise. She hissed at me through clenched teeth as I scrubbed the sooty old cast iron frying pan she used: "Don't you dare tell anyone I learned this on the farm in Silesia." She had picked the apples that had fallen under a big tree right in the middle of the village and the onions were a gift from none other than Herr Schinkel. He had an eye for pretty women and had tried more than once to grab our behinds. I always slapped his hand, which seemed to delight him. I knew it was no use to pick a row now. Quarreling with one of our suppliers would only delay my trip to Munich for the longed-for passport.

Luke became more and more interesting to me. He came from Hannibal, Missouri but considered himself a "progressive," not at all, he told me, like those "homosexuals with their 4F exemptions" from his hometown or the guys in his "meatball platoon." When I asked him what a meatball was as applied to a man, he found my ignorance charming and kissed me lightly on the mouth. For a split second I had the feeling I had come to know well as the prelude to sexual longing. But I was quite adept at pushing it down, very aware that I loved neither Luke nor Uwe. Luke defined a meatball man as someone who oafishly obeys orders and is faithful unto death. I looked at him with all the disdain I could muster and declared: "I would expect my man to be faithful to me unto death." At which point he nearly drowned me with kisses, undone by my delightful lack of knowledge. To divert Luke's attention, I burbled on about the coincidence of a small town in the United States being named for an ancient Carthaginian general.

Even before I had received my passport, I thought it wise to continue my friendship with Luke. He might come in handy with advice on how to get to the United States. Little did I anticipate just how appreciative Luke would become, though he became grumpy at my diversionary tactics. Perhaps, I thought, what Walt said about Mother was true of me: "A charming tease that can make a man weak in the knees." And so I smiled and giggled and talked about the general named Hannibal who crossed the Alps, so I thought, with a bunch of elephants. At which point Luke turned purple, got up, and gunned his jeep out of town. I was afraid I had lost him and my chance for a friend in New York or Hannibal, Missouri, when I finally got there. When I confessed my worries to Uwe the next day, he put his arms around me and proved to be a wonderful kisser who did not want to suck me into him or drown me in saliva.

I was thoroughly enjoying myself when my little brother appeared and, instead of staring and pestering us, shouted a message at me. Mother and Dad wanted me home immediately, *toute suite*. Our postwar wanderings had left us all multilingual, as we imitated the speech of GIs, who in turn adapted certain French and German phrases to suit themselves. I wrestled myself free from Uwe, who quickly straightened Walt's cravat and gallantly offered to walk me home. He was taking this summons very personally, thinking that we would be forbidden to see each other.

When I arrived I saw Luke's jeep parked in the middle of the entrance road, blocking all traffic. I was surprised because Luke was as careful with what he called "government issue" as he was romantically sloppy about his person. (However, he did use a wonderful aftershave lotion.) As a precaution, I sent Uwe away and entered my parents' domain with shaking knees. What did they have in mind? Would they forbid me from obtaining my passport?

My mother threw herself at me like a tigress. "You little whore," she hissed. "To think that an honorable man wants to marry you and at your age . . ." She slammed out of the door, dragging my little brother with her. "Why is she a whowho? What's a whowho?" he wailed.

Walt and Luke sat opposite each other, obviously having had a satisfactory man-to-man talk. Walt beckoned to me, and I faced the two sitting males like a potential criminal. Shocked into near immobility, every nerve raw and quivering, I forced myself to smile. "What is she talking about?" I asked as civilly as I could.

Walt looked less grim than Luke. "The lieutenant has asked for your hand in marriage. I told him you have no dowry, nothing. And, of course, you are much too young, though if what your mother thinks is true . . ."

Luke nodded vigorously and remarked, "She has herself." He got up and once again I was in his grip. My mother returned. "He," she pointed at Luke, "has agreed to take you as his wife. Despite . . . my God, the plans I had for you and now this!"

Luke stroked my hair. "Do you sometimes think how it will be when you are my wife in Hannibal?" "No, absolutely not," I stammered. "I want to go to America." "You little fool, that's where we will live, of course," Luke reassured me. "Your mother is just upset because she thinks I want to marry you because we did . . . you know." "Know what?" I yelled. "We . . . I didn't do anything."

"Don't lie to me, you brazen hussy," Mother carried on. "Someone more trustworthy than you, an adult woman, saw you in your filthy behavior."

"Now, wait a minute," I replied as Luke's triumph was waning. "What do you mean? Whom did she see?" He let go of me. Lieselotte's mother and her binoculars presented themselves full blown in my mind. "When are we going to Munich to get my passport?" I asked and sat down next to Walt. I wanted to remind them of what was important. My passport, I knew, would give me my freedom, the privilege to travel and to leave these tiresome meddlers. Luke had already left.

Shortly before Walt and I left for Munich, Mother had made a trip of her own. One of her contacts at the local American army headquarters had introduced her to our military governor, a regular army man who had just recently received a promotion to lieutenant colonel. She wore her best dove grey suit for her appointment with him but matched her oldest "clodhoppers" with it. She added a wide brimmed hat that had become dented and lost its shape in the rain. All in all, she gave the impression of dethroned and slightly shopworn royalty. She shot me a slightly conspiratorial look when she left.

I thought she was going to apply for travel permits for both of us, but when I saw her outfit I knew something unforeseen was afoot. Uwe put it into perspective for me. "She is going to seduce him," he declared. "She had no right to talk to you like that." He looked so grim I became worried that he too wanted to be responsible and marry me.

Uwe continued his shy and tender approaches, which left me free to talk of my dream of going to America and finding my biological father. "I wish I could go with you," he sighed. "You can," I generously decided. "American citizens can bring over their families. We'll get married when I have my passport and then we'll go."

Uwe's expression became darker: "I was an officer candidate, remember? They won't give me a visa. And what would we live on? It takes money to go to America." I assured him I wasn't worried. We would get the money somehow. Hadn't he somehow gotten money for his new trousers when he was making only a few marks a month as an office trainee in Walt's group? He sighed again: "The source will dry up if she realizes what the money is for."

Suddenly I understood. Lieselotte's mother had not yet finished with Uwe. It was she who had spied on me and given Mother the wrong impression. For the first time, I felt a need to speak to Luke. Maybe he had slobbered all over me because he believed he loved me, without my girlfriend's mother thrusting her body between us. And he did want to marry me, and as an officer he surely made more money than Uwe. Maybe I would have to begin my life in America in Hannibal, Missouri after all.

Mother was successful with Lieutenant Colonel McClintock. He invited her to a celebration of his new rank, which she accepted over Walt's objection. She protested and reminded him that she wanted to go to Berlin to salvage what she could of their belongings. "If the victors carried on there like here, there won't be much left," he demurred. "They don't know a Persian rug even when they walk on one, and they spell antique with a *k*, she remarked scornfully of her otherwise adored Americans. "I'll be able to get a lot out."

We had heard vague rumors that the city, sitting in the middle of what would become East Germany, was to be cut into quarters. It seemed like an impossible scheme, but we all lived through the impossible. Walt thought of the desk that had belonged to his great grandfather, of the rugs his brother had brought back from his travels in Arabia, of his great grandmother's china. Maybe some of it had survived the bombing. People were stirring a bit out of their depressing disillusionment with Hitler's thousand year empire. Their rage at having once again lost a war gave them incentive to best the victors in a thousand little ways, like rescuing their beloved furniture. I noted that the people who thought of themselves as better educated and less materialistic than their American conquerors invariably "did something" about their possessions, rarely the possessions of other people. "Doing something" had become a catch phase of the day.

So mother, the perennial doer, did something once more. She managed somehow to go to Berlin and stage a rescue operation that was the envy of all who learned about it. A British truck arrived with many of our belongings intact. In the ensuing melee about what to store where, my dilemma was forgotten. But not by me. Despite the many unkind remarks I heard about my mother's "talents," I had borrowed a page from her book and tried to become close to her "like a mother and daughter should be." But, looking back, I see that she would have none of it. Nothing I said convinced her that I was still intact like her furniture. If I had given up Uwe, maybe that would have convinced her, but I had no intention of doing so.

We never put the situation into words until Uwe himself one day suggested that he would rather be with someone closer to his age. He was doing all right in his job and had received promotions. I wasn't clear on the nature of his promotion, but he suddenly stopped supporting my dream of going to America. He wanted to stay in Germany. I didn't respond but decided to contact Luke after all, something I had talked myself out of before. All these adults seemed like liars to me, but how could I be surprised given what was going on all over at national, local, familial, and individual levels.

But how to find Luke? It was a good five miles to where the army had quartered him and, though I had no doubt that I could walk far, I had no idea exactly where his apartment was. The few times I had been there, I was overcome by emotion and only had eyes for him. Even when his two roommates appeared, I took no notice of my whereabouts. It had been so rare to be alone with him, with neither chaperones nor hordes of little boys following us around. I figured now that it would take me all day to find him, confront him, and then come back. I was confident I would know exactly what to say when I faced him. Even going to Hannibal, Missouri would be better than staying in Germany.

But a future with Luke in the American Midwest was not in the cards for me. In the end, I left for America unencumbered and on no one's arm. Despite my mother's ongoing protests, the passport and visa were procured and the date of my departure arranged. Walt convinced my mother to accept my biological father's offer of $200 to cover the fare for my return trip to the U.S. This was a sum that, according to the U.S. Consulate, would insure my passage on *Liberty*, a military vessel. I was deeply moved by the offer and was even given permission to write to him. It took six weeks for the letter to be delivered. With no thought of either Uwe or Luke, I looked ahead to my new life. I had no sense of leaving anything behind and thought only of what lay before me.

chapter fourteen
ARRIVAL

I don't think I'll ever forget that day. It was one of those heartbreakingly soft sunny days one only learns to appreciate much later in life. But there I was, 17 years old but feeling quite old and wise. Hadn't I survived the most horrible of wars, and what's more, hadn't I lived through and past my mother's ferocious Munchhausen fantasies? For one black moment I felt her presence; she was still on my back. Then I relaxed. There she was: Lady Liberty. Another fantasy rescued me from the doomsday scenario of my first feeling. I imagined Lady Liberty wrapped in a mantel of flowers, holding aloft a cornucopia of fruit instead of a torch and wearing a Greek Olympian's wreath rather than those spikes on which a person might be mortally impaled. How could I know that one day one of my children would have her replica as an ornament on her wedding cake, alongside a William Tell figure signifying her husband's Swiss nationality. Standing on the deck at 17, I could only imagine my own future – a future in which I could finally do what I wanted: to dance, to be in theater, to allow myself to be Elaine. I felt whole again.

It was utterly intoxicating. No more curtsies to old ladies in faded black silk dresses who smelled of camphor and sherry. No more feeling inferior because I had no title and was the Jewish child of a German divorcee and an American. But most intoxicating of all: to be an American, to be on the side of the victors. What untold adventures lay before me. I felt my body expanding with glee. I laughed and cried and wasn't afraid to show emotion that some might have thought unladylike.

I had come to Lady Liberty in a tiny cabin on a small liberty ship that, without stabilizer, crossed an angry Atlantic for ten days. I shared my cabin with another teenager, Kate, and she seemed to be feeling the same as I. We were packed together on deck, crowding each other in an effort to see the statue. Even the dozen or so young Polish Orthodox Jews had been permitted by their rabbi, himself a pale and morose teenager, to come out and *daven* (chant prayers) in the Lady's presence.

They must have seen our astonishment that they had come on deck. During the long journey they had made it quite clear that we were to stay away from their spiritual leader, a holy youth who was the scion of a distinguished rabbinical family and had survived to help them to peace. They had not been pious enough, they believed, so the Almighty, blessed be He, had punished them with atrocities and the concentration camps.

I had never met anyone like them before and felt old antagonisms rising up, the kind that prompt you to defend against all feelings. Now, on deck, they surrounded their holy youth, put their *tallithim* (prayer shawls) around their shoulders and davened as one. Too bad, I thought. They will have to learn better. But would they? I liked them as little as they liked me.

But here was Kate, my new friend, and my unknown father would be at the pier to greet me. I hadn't seen him since I was two years old. But I was too taken up with visions of how I would create my new life to worry about an unknown father who had quite willingly sent many care packages and now the money for my voyage.

A number of people were awaiting my arrival, but I had left behind in Germany my mother, my stepfather, my half-brother and all my grandparents. Opa Ferdinand Schwager made it his mission to look for his wife, my Oma Anna, at the end of the war. Eventually he found her in the files of the medical corps attached to a research unit of the Luftwaffe and knew for certain she had been killed. We were given to understand that she had received a lethal injection and took what solace we could in the knowledge she had passed quickly and without pain. I would write Opa Ferdinand often, but not as often as I wrote my mother, who received a weekly letter. Across the continents, in our letters and occasional phone calls, we mourned together this wonderful woman. Sadly, our memories of Oma Anna seemed all that bound us together.

But on that day of soft sunshine in 1946, with Lady Liberty beckoning and my new friend Kate by my side, feelings of what I had left behind were drowned out by feelings of what lay before me. With the extraordinary strength and empowering attitude of the young, I gave way to reveries of the future. The present was mine and always would be. Another young woman joined us. She too wore that look of having learned far more than she should have over the course of her young life. The three of us looked at one other and felt a kinship. We were all so wise and so heartbreakingly young and destined to be friends forever in our America.

Elaine V. Siegel

ABOUT THE AUTHOR

Now in retirement after a long and distinguished career as both a psychoanalyst and registered dance therapist, Elaine V. Siegel is widely published in both German and English and has lectured extensively in the United States and Europe. Her text *Tanztherapie* (Dance Therapy) was widely used in Germany for many years. Formerly training and supervising analyst at the New York Center for Psychoanalytic Training and Director of the Motor Development Unit at Suffolk Child Development Center (State University of New York, Stony Brook), she now resides in Wayland, MA.

www.ingramcontent.com/pod-product-compliance
Lightning Source LLC
Chambersburg PA
CBHW020948230426
43666CB00005B/225